DECK
IDEAS THAT WORK

DECK
IDEAS THAT WORK

PETER JESWALD

The Taunton Press

The Taunton Press
Inspiration for hands-on living®

The Taunton Press, Inc.,
63 South Main Street, PO Box 5506,
Newtown, CT 06470-5506
e-mail: tp@taunton.com

Copy editor: Diane Sinitsky
Interior design: Carol Petro
Layout: David Giammattei
Illustrator: Christine Erikson
Cover Photographers: (Front cover, clockwise from top): Chris Giles; Eric Roth; Eric Roth; courtesy of Trex®; Eric Roth;
(Back cover, clockwise from top): www.kenricephoto.com; courtesy of Correct Deck; Chris Giles; courtesy of Bison;
courtesy of Lawrence Winterburn, builder, Garden Structures; Eric Roth

Library of Congress Cataloging-in-Publication Data
Jeswald, Peter.
  Deck ideas that work / Peter Jeswald.
      p. cm. -- (Ideas that work)
  ISBN 978-1-60085-372-2 (pbk.)
  1. Decks (Architecture, Domestic)–Design and construction. I. Title.
  TH4970.J469 2012
  690'.893--dc23
                                    2011034960

Printed in the United States of America
10 9 8 7 6 5 4 3 2 1

The following names/manufacturers appearing in *Deck Ideas That Work* are trademarks: Advantage™ Trim and Lumber; Archadeck®;
AstroTURF®; Backyard America™; Chief Architect®; Deckorators®; Feeney® Architectural Products; Kalamazoo™ Outdoor Gourmet;
Sketchup™; Total 3D™; Trex®.

ACKNOWLEDGMENTS

I begin by thanking Jessica DiDonato, editor at The Taunton Press, who was a pleasure to collaborate with and who worked tirelessly to shepherd this book from start to finish.

I also thank the following people for taking time out of their busy schedules to answer my questions and share their knowledge and insights: Dave Petersen, Outdoor Structure Company, LLC; Lawrence Winterburn, GardenStructure.com; Bobby Parks, Peachtree Decks and Porches, LLC; Jim Hawkins, building commissioner for the Franklin County Cooperative Inspection Program; and my good friend, David Vreeland, Vreeland Associates.

CONTENTS

INTRODUCTION

Every year across the country, millions of homeowners share something in common—they add a deck to their home. The number of decks built each year—approximately 3 million—is astounding, particularly when you consider that decks are a relatively new component of the American home. As late as the 1950s, few homes sported decks. However, as the American lifestyle became more informal, flat building lots became less available, and people's desire to spend more time outdoors increased, residential decks found their place in the sun. In fact, of all the spaces in their homes, many homeowners name the deck as their favorite. In warmer climates, decks might even be the most frequently inhabited area of the home.

In retrospect, it's easy to see why decks became such a popular way to add living space. Because they are constructed outside, building a deck causes minimal disruptions in day-to-day living. Decks can be faster and cheaper to build than hand-laid patios and on steeply sloping sites may be the only reasonable option for creating outdoor living space.

However, perhaps because they are so common, decks can be taken for granted. All too often decks appear to be a mere afterthought, something that's mindlessly tacked on to the back of a house. But because they are important living spaces, decks deserve the time and thoughtful attention you would give to planning an interior space such as a kitchen or bathroom. That's where *Deck Ideas That Work* can help. It provides you with the important information you need and inspirational examples to get your juices flowing to help you create a deck that exceeds your dreams.

Filled with photographs of beautiful, functional decks, *Deck Ideas That Work* begins by introducing you to the most popular uses for decks to get you thinking about what you ultimately want from your outdoor space. Then you'll explore the types of decks you might build to suit those uses as well as fit with your home and landscape. Naturally, the necessary steps to successfully plan your deck are laid out. Equally important to proper planning is detailed information about the various materials and components—decking, railings, stairs, fasteners—that comprise a properly designed and well-built deck. *Deck Ideas That Work* ends with a chapter on how to outfit your deck with furniture, decor, and accessories for maximum enjoyment.

Keep in mind that nuggets of information can be found throughout, so be sure to read through the entire book, even if a section or type of deck doesn't appeal to you. Whether you'd like somewhere to cook outdoors, a place for dining under the sun, a spot to soak in a hot tub under the stars, or a quiet outdoor retreat, you'll find a deck that fits you, your lifestyle, and your home perfectly.

ENVISIONING

The wonderful thing about decks is that they extend living space into the great outdoors. For the most part, any activity you can do inside can also be done outside, so how would you like to use your deck?

YOUR DECK

Make a Wish List

Have you ever found yourself looking wistfully out your kitchen window, longing for a place to linger under the sun with your morning coffee? Perhaps you're fed up with that narrow set of steps that dumps you unceremoniously on your lawn with no place to go. Maybe you'd like an informal space where your family and friends can hang out and not worry about overturned glasses and crumbs underfoot. Do you enjoy entertaining and covet an outdoor space where your friends can enjoy fun-filled summer evenings? How about a place to take a warm soak in a tub or a cool dip in a pool? Could you use a private retreat where your only company is the sun, the breeze, and the view? Would you like to welcome your guests with a new front entry? Well, a new deck may just be the answer to your dreams.

Before you jump to any premature conclusions about your future deck, take some time to thoroughly investigate all of your options. To begin, clip pictures from magazines, download information from the Internet, and snap photos of decks you like. Your goal is to uncover and consider as many ideas and options as possible. As you do, organize all of your findings in folders and keep notes to help you remember the features you really like so that you can review them as you start to design your deck. To help make this process more fun, pretend for the time being that money is no object and that you can afford, and have, anything you see or want. Setting and adhering to a budget certainly has its place but not here, not yet.

It's been my experience that one person is typically the driving force behind most construction projects. Perhaps that person has more time, understands the needs of the family better, or has a particular craving. However, a successful process is usually inclusive, and if you are the motivated member of your family, part of your job is to get everyone on board. If you

above · Opening onto an expansive backyard, this deck has ample space on which to enjoy multiple activities, including lounging, dining, and soaking in the hot tub. When the conversation extends into the evening or a rain shower passes through, everyone can adjourn to the large, screened gazebo.

left · Feel like sitting in a cozy love seat for two, enjoying a meal with friends, or kicking back, putting up your feet, and reading the latest thriller? Then here's the deck for you. With its multiple and varied seating groupings, this deck not only accommodates different pursuits but also your shifting moods. A unique feature is the sitting bench that morphs into a plant shelf.

above · Although you might not have an ocean view from your backyard, there's probably an out-of-the-way corner where you could build a deck and dream of tropical breezes and gently rolling waves. This private deck is shaped to fit around the existing plants, and its simple forms and uniform grey color are soothing. A nearby hammock completes the mood.

have trouble generating interest, try organizing a family brainstorming session. Set up some guidelines before you begin. For example, everyone's opinion carries equal weight; everyone is to be supportive and encouraging; there is no such thing as a bad idea; and try to build on someone else's ideas.

After brainstorming, ask everyone in your family to create his or her own wish list. Include the ideas and information from the session and earlier research. Divide the list into two columns: one for types of spaces/activities and the other for kinds of accessories. It's also important to establish a "sequence of surrender," prioritizing the lists from the top down, from the most to the least important. That way, when the inevitable budget constraints make an appearance, they will shorten your list from the bottom up.

After all is said and done, you'll have identified what type of deck is best suited for you and your family.

Dining and Cooking

The two most popular types of decks are probably those used for dining and cooking. Perhaps we have our prehistoric ancestors to thank, or maybe it's the fond childhood memories of eating s'mores around the campfire, but there seems to be something alluring about eating and cooking outdoors. Nostalgia may be in play here, but there are also some practical reasons. Grilling and smoking food, two tasty cooking methods, are best done outdoors, and when the cooking is finished and the meal is over, cleanup is less of a chore.

above · **One of the great things about a grill is its portability. For easy access to diners, the grill is located right next to the table. But if the chef needs more room, he or she can wheel the grill to another location. And since this cooking and dining area is elevated, there is no chance that moving the grill will disrupt activities going on in other areas of the deck.**

above right · **The protection afforded by the overhead cover allows the outdoor chef to keep cooking even if Mother Nature didn't get the memo requesting fair skies. The dining area is located away from the kitchen, at the other end of the deck, which can be a plus during those times when the table is upwind from the grilling smoke.**

right · **In addition to the usual kitchen equipment, this full-service kitchen, which is aligned along one side of the deck, boasts an unusual beehive oven. A conveniently located and ample counter serves the oven and the countertop grill, which is large enough to keep the food coming for even the hungriest crowd.**

FAMILY DINING

One of the challenges of fast-paced, modern living is getting the family together for a sit-down meal. A deck designed for family dining, coupled with the novelty of eating outdoors, may be just the lure you need to gather everyone together. There are some keys to making sure your family dining deck works the magic you desire.

Locate a family dining deck as close as possible to either the inside kitchen or dining room. This is important because putting the deck a mere step or two away reduces the potential of inertia—the tendency for family members to want to stay put—foiling your plans for outdoor dining. It also makes it less of a chore to run back and forth to the house when you forget to bring out the ketchup or relish.

Do things that allow your deck to be ready for a meal at the drop of a hat. For example, consider having a special set of "outdoor" tableware and store it, if possible, near the door that leads to the deck. Include items such as napkins, salt and pepper shakers, and trivets, in addition to plates, glasses, and silverware. A few nonslip trays will help ferry these accoutrements efficiently.

Don't let your eye for efficiency stop at the door. To complement the requisite table and chairs (see pp. 163–174), outfit your deck with some additional furniture. It's a universal truth that there never seems to be enough surfaces upon which to put things. Small tables and rolling carts will keep the dining table clear of clutter by providing convenient places to put serving dishes, drink pitchers, and condiments. If a portion of your deck will be protected from the rain, consider storing the tableware in an outdoor cabinet. It might take a bit more time to put the dishes there after they are washed, but that's minor compared with the advantage of having them close at hand at mealtime.

left · Situated a few steps outside the door, the dining table, which is easily visible through the glass, beckons. Although set for two, the lightweight aluminum and mesh fabric chairs can be moved into place easily when guests drop by.

below · The dining area on this deck is clearly delineated by its octagonal shape and decking pattern. An efficient L-shaped kitchen is far enough away to separate the cooking and eating functions, but not so distant that food will get cold while it's being transported from the grill to the table.

COOKING

Cooking food outdoors goes hand-in-hand with outdoor dining. Although it has universal appeal, it may be an occasional activity for some and an all-consuming passion for others. Whether cooking outdoors means allotting a little space for a small grill or creating a complete outdoor kitchen, there are a number of things you can do to make the experience successful.

As with outdoor dining, location is important. If the only piece of cooking equipment will be a grill, the grilling area should be positioned as close as possible to the kitchen so it can take advantage of the kitchen's "support services," such as the sink and refrigerator. Be careful, however, that you don't locate the grill too close to a door or an operable window because greasy smoke could easily be blown in its direction. Consider the direction of the prevailing breezes—often from the south during the grilling season—and the wind patterns around your house, and locate the grill far enough away so that the smoke is pushed to the side of, or rises over, the house. A fully equipped outdoor kitchen is more self-sufficient and, as a result, its location can be influenced more by traffic flow and its relationship to the other parts of the deck and the landscape.

When planning for grill-only outdoor cooking, you should designate a specific area on the deck for the grill, whether the grill will be movable or fixed. For this reason, it's important to determine how large a grill you will want and allocate space accordingly (see p. 103). Although many grills sport wide shelves, there often doesn't seem to be adequate counter space for platters of meats and veggies. One approach is to build the grill into a fixed counter or utilize portable tables and carts. Another option is to purchase a modular grilling station. Most have counters and cabinet storage and some come with under-counter refrigerators.

In addition to a grill, a true outdoor kitchen has all the equipment found in its indoor cousin—cooking surface, oven, refrigerator, sink, and dishwasher. A full-service outdoor kitchen should enable the chef to prepare the entire meal and even do some of the cleanup on the deck. Of course, some of this equipment requires utility hookups, such as electricity, water, and fuel (natural gas or propane). Keep in mind that the cost of installing utilities goes up as the distance between the house and outdoor kitchen increases.

The guidelines for designing an outdoor kitchen—the work triangle and adequate counter and storage space—are generally the same as for an indoor kitchen. One important decision is how much "help" you want in your outdoor kitchen. Plan accordingly by either providing adequate space around the kitchen or ways to keep the helpers out.

Having an outdoor kitchen or grilling station also influences your decking choices. Splattering meats, dripping marinades, and dropped plates all cause grease spills, an inevitable part of cooking. To minimize the severity of grease stains, choose a decking material for cooking areas that resists stains and is easy to clean up.

above right • With the right accessories, a basic grill can turn out an al fresco feast fit for a king. Stone pillars mark this grill-sized 45-degree corner, and a pair of large earthenware planters further define the cooking space.

right • This kitchen packs a lot—smoker, grill, wine cooler, and sink—into a small footprint. Flipping the location of the grill and smoker would have lessened the possibility of smoke getting into the house and shortened the length of the water piping to the sink.

far right • Installed in substantial stone and a tile counter, the grill and adjacent deep fat fryer stand ready to prepare meals for nearby diners on the deck or at the picnic table on the lawn. Lighting built into the backsplash illuminates the counter after the sun has set.

Grill Safety

The open flames and grease associated with cooking on a grill can present a significant fire risk. Here are some simple guidelines to reduce the risk of fire.

- Use propane and charcoal grills outdoors only.
- Keep at least 2 ft. of clearance from flammable structures such as wood siding and railings.
- Don't locate your grill underneath low, overhanging trees.
- To prevent dangerous flare-ups, clean your grill regularly to keep grease from building up on the grates.
- Never leave your grill unattended.
- Consider installing a fireproof mat underneath your grill, especially if it is a charcoal grill.
- Use and store starter fluids and electric charcoal starters properly.

Outdoor Kitchen Equipment

A full-service outdoor kitchen enables the al fresco chef to prepare the entire meal outside, but that requires a full complement of kitchen equipment. Luckily, that's not a problem because appliance manufacturers offer a wide assortment of equipment that's designed specifically for outdoor use.

Even if you're mainly a grill-only cook, you might want to consider branching out by adding one or two of these options.

1. Just tilt the door and toss in your trash. This is a great way to keep the trash bin out of sight yet convenient. **2.** Here's an appliance for the true beer aficionado—a double-drawer refrigerator for holding bottled or canned beer, plus a refrigerated keg compartment complete with a pull tap. **3.** A high-rise faucet makes it easy to fill a tall pot or rinse garden greens. Choosing a model with a swing arm provides additional flexibility. **4.** This double-door beverage cooler has ample room for white wine, soda, or beer, and the glass front puts your thirst-quenching options in plain sight. **5.** For those times when you want to boil a big pot of water for corn or pasta, or simmer a basting sauce near your grill, this self-contained cooktop unit fills the bill. **6.** A wood-fired pizza oven produces a crust that can't be beat. This unit has a convenient, built-in wood storage compartment. **7.** Nothing tastes quite like smoked meats, and a smoker box will let you make this delicacy along with your grilled foods.

4

5

6

7

Entertaining

If you enjoy hosting large parties or your house is the setting for frequent family gatherings, a deck designed for entertaining can be a great addition to your home, and it also might spare wear and tear on its interior. Decks intended for entertaining should accommodate at least three activities—dining, cooking, and lounging. Although its size depends on the number of people it's intended to hold, to function properly, a deck for entertaining will typically be larger than a single-use deck.

Although location is also a consideration for an entertainment deck, the relationship of the three activities is perhaps more important because of the deck's large size and multiple functions. For example, if the deck will stretch along the length of the house, one approach would be to put the cooking area at one end, the sitting area at the other, and join the two together with the dining area—even if this doesn't coincide with the interior floor plan. This arrangement separates the more hectic and potentially smoky cooking area from one intended to be more relaxing. If the deck will be an L shape, a good solution is to locate the kitchen at the end of the L and the dining and sitting areas against the house. In both of these scenarios, access from the house to the deck could be at the dining area.

When planning furniture layout, take into consideration that people tend to gather in small groups at social events, so rather than creating one large seating group, create several smaller ones. While some folks like to be right in the middle of things, others prefer to be on the periphery, so be sure to plan for some seating off to the side. And for those who want to be close to the action, some type of seating—high stools, perhaps—adjacent to the cooking area might be appropriate.

Outdoor entertaining usually includes providing something to eat. If your gatherings are typically informal, plan guest seating accordingly. In addition to the dining table, provide small tables at every seating group so that your guests don't have to balance their plates on their knees. For sit-down meals, make sure that your table is large enough for everyone you've invited. Alternately, choose a square or rectangular style so that you can easily add another table or two at one end.

Easy access to and from the house and several different seating groups ensure that guests will find their way to, and linger on, a deck. Wooden furniture can be heavy to move, but lightweight metal can easily slide over to join another conversation.

A Well-Designed Entertaining Deck

Paying attention to the organization and relationships of the different spaces on your deck is essential for maximum usability. For example, reversing the position of the kitchen and dining areas on this deck would have isolated diners from the more compatible sitting and lounging areas and put the kitchen activity too close to the "quieter zones."

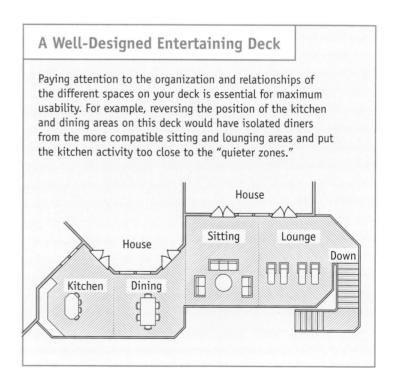

The mature plantings, brick and stucco walls of the house, and metal furniture give this deck a decidedly old-world feel and set the stage for quiet gatherings. The low stone wall can be used for informal seating, and the row of torches will cast a warm glow over the guests.

A Cool Place to Entertain

The owners of this lovely, two-story southern home entertain frequently and wanted to take advantage of the long outdoor season by moving some of their social activities to their secluded backyard. However, the small, square deck initially located there was anything but inviting, and the sun, which bore down relentlessly, made matters worse. The owners developed a two-part plan to remedy the situation.

First, with the help of their builder, they designed a large deck with ample room for sitting and dining, which includes a bump-out for the grill and a lovely breakfast bar. One crucial, owner-envisioned feature—a pergola—is located over the sitting area to fend off the blazing sun and keep the lounge area cool and relaxing. Another focal point, a broad set of steps lead to the second component—a rejuvenated landscape that lies between their deck and new in-ground pool.

above right • Located under the pergola, the conversation area takes advantage of the shade and the cooling breeze generated by the overhead fan. The furniture is pulled away from the wall to allow traffic to easily pass behind it.

right • Bumping out a small portion of the deck to accommodate the grill keeps it out of the way yet conveniently located and maintains the spacious feeling of the generously proportioned dining area. Extra seating can be added in the form of bar stools along the wide-topped railing to the right of the dining table.

Viewed from the swimming pool, the deck's pergola provides much-needed shade. Its horizontal line echoes the small roof to the left and breaks up the tall rear elevation.

Hot Tubs and Pools

After a hard day at work, running errands, or chasing after children, who wouldn't want to sink shoulder-deep in a hot tub or spa? Or how about a few laps in a pool to work that tension out of your body? A deck that incorporates one or both of these enjoyable items can help you lose your worries and, who knows, might just add a few years to your life.

Decks for hot tubs and pools must be large enough to not only accommodate them but also the people who gather and the activities that take place around them (see p. 103). People spend as much, if not more, time outside the water than in it, so take that into account during the planning process. If the pool or tub deck will be some distance from the house, consider providing space for a grill, counters for serving drinks and snacks, and some storage.

below • At first glance it might seem that two sets of steps so close together, each leading to the pool, might be overkill, but closer inspection reveals the reason. The steps to the left give direct access from the house to the pool and adjacent sitting area, while the right-side steps lead straight to the hot tub.

left · Connections to water and capturing the sun are the themes behind this multilevel, articulated deck. While sitting in the shade is a pleasure on hot days, so is jumping in the pool and sunbathing afterwards, which is why much of the deck is positioned out in the yard and away from the shadows.

below · This seating area and grilling station overlook the hot tub and in-ground pool, allowing those who are "deck-side" to keep an ear and an eye on water activities.

Hot Tub and Pool Safety

You won't be able to fully relax unless you know that your water-activity deck is safe. Hot tubs and swimming pools all share the same potential drowning danger to young children. National and local codes typically specify the need for and type of security barriers to make them safer, but even if those codes are not in place in your area, you should take it upon yourself to make them a part of your deck. Check with your local building inspector about safety requirements.

HOT TUBS

Hot tubs and jetted spas are small enough so that they can fit on most moderate-sized decks, but before you make a snap judgment, wave your arm, and say, "Yeah, let's put the hot tub over there, somewhere," stop and give it some careful thought. As with most decks, location is a prime concern, and your desire for privacy will heavily influence your decision. Do you want the tub or spa to be a focal point of your deck, or would you prefer a more discreet position for your hot-water haven? Either way, investigate the lines of sight from the house, other portions of the deck, and the neighbor's property, and plan accordingly.

Hot tubs and spas are frequently used at night, when privacy can feel even more important. You'll need to provide adequate lighting so that you can get to the tub safely but not so much light that it feels like a stage. Utilizing multiple switches and dimmers can allow you to adjust the light to create the appropriate mood. If your nighttime sky is dark enough, the view from the spa will shift toward the heavens. To be able to see the rising moon or the Milky Way, don't position your spa under the view-blocking canopy of a tall tree.

This artistically detailed pergola shelters and defines the hot tub area below. Those using the hot tub can still enjoy the view, which is not obscured by the glass-panel railings.

above · Although low, the pair of planters and accompanying storage bench creates just enough separation from the seating to give the hot tub its own sense of place.

above · The privacy screens and subdued lighting make this hot tub the perfect place for a romantic, midnight soak. Even though the tub is relatively out of the way, the door to the house is only a few steps away.

left · This pool is unusual in that it was constructed on top of the deck, requiring careful engineering and a beefed-up structure for additional support. In an elegant touch, the end of the deck is curved to match the shape of the hot tub.

Hot-Tub Heaven

When you have a breathtaking view, why not take full advantage of it? That's exactly what this stunning hot-tub deck does. Perched on a rocky promontory, this small deck packs a visual wallop and makes the most out of the limited available space. If you're feeling adventurous, you can walk right up to the metal railing and take in the view. Those who are a bit squeamish about heights can sit or even lie down on the generous bench and bask in the sun. And there's plenty of room around the hot tub to sit on its edge and soak your feet.

Strategically placed behind a high back and stone and wooden walls, this slightly curved bench provides a comfortable place to change before or after enjoying the tub. A generous storage bin provides ample room for cushions, towels, and yoga mats.

Although the stone walls that surround this deck may hide what's behind it, the simple yet elegant metal gate welcomes you and hints at what lies ahead. The gate and walls also serve a practical function by meeting the code that requires spas and pools to be protected by fences.

These wedge-shaped steps lead you toward the hot tub but also give you other options—move to the left toward the view or to the right to the "sunning" portion of the deck.

POOLS

Swimming pools, both above-ground and in-ground, are so large that their location is often dictated by the shape and topography of the yard. In fact, for this reason, many pools and the decks constructed around them are separated from the house. While building a deck is the only viable way to create space around an above-ground swimming pool, in-ground pools are typically associated with stone or concrete patios, but decks do have some advantages.

On a sloping site, because a deck doesn't have to be constructed directly on the ground, it may reduce the amount of necessary excavation and grading compared to that needed for a patio. Some folks prefer the softer look of a wood or synthetic surface, and it's certainly softer underfoot and easier on the knees of stumbling children. Wood decking is cooler underfoot than many patio materials.

Positioning a Pool

As you create a design for your pool and accompanying deck, be sure to orient both with the sun and surrounding view in mind.

- Pools are typically used in the afternoon hours, so in most areas of the country they should have a southern to southwestern exposure to capture the afternoon sun.
- In hotter climates, if it's possible, you may want to orient the pool so that a portion of the deck is shaded by overhanging trees, or you can provide ample shade with umbrellas or overhead structures.
- Consider what views or areas of the yard you'd like to see from the pool deck, and orient the seating areas accordingly.
- If you don't have a gorgeous distant view, spruce up the landscape around your home or orient the seating toward the house.

above and right · This deck obscures the fact that the pool, constructed on a sloping site, is partially in-ground and partially above-ground. Although they are located relatively far from the house, the dining and sitting areas adjacent to the pool are situated to take advantage of the distant views. The pergola and multiple ceiling fans help to keep people cool while enjoying lunch and the view during the heat of the day. The integral fanlights encourage the festivities to continue into the night.

facing page · Completely surrounded by a deck, this above-ground pool looks very much like its much costlier in-ground counterpart. The step up to the pool deck is a nice touch, and the alternating-board fence creates privacy and echoes the pattern of the wooden decking.

Retreats

Let's face it, sometimes we all need to physically separate ourselves from our surroundings and get away from it all. When there's no time to jump in the car and drive somewhere, a private, out-of-the-way deck can be the perfect retreat. Of course, it's relatively easy to achieve the desired effect in a rural setting and spacious landscape, but it's also possible in a large, or even modest, suburban yard—it just takes a little more creativity. Once again, choosing the proper location is key.

Your first impulse may be to choose the spot in your yard that is the farthest from your house or the neighbors', but this might not be the best option. Rather, look for a place that's the easiest in which to create a sense of privacy. For example, locate your private deck near a seldom-used portion of the house or a side that has few windows. A solid, stockade type of fence is a good way to shield your deck from the neighbors' sight, but unless you build a very tall fence, views from their second-story window can be difficult to block. However, if your deck is tucked right up against the fence, the neighbors' line of sight will be over the top and you'll be happily hidden. Employing an overhead structure, such as a pergola, is another way to block second-story views.

To create more privacy, you could surround your deck with fences, but it might end up feeling more like a prison than a retreat. Closely spaced bushes and small trees can create an effective screen, but be sure to choose varieties that keep their lower branches and retain their leaves or needles for all or most of the year. Of course, the view from your deck is also important, so carefully orient the seating to take advantage of desirable views and avoid unwanted ones.

What will you do on your deck—read, practice yoga, meditate? Sound, whether originating from your family, your neighbors, or a nearby street, can be intrusive and compromise the effect you want to achieve with your deck retreat. Short of wearing earplugs, you probably won't be able to completely silence the noise, but a solid fence can help here, too. Sound does not like to turn corners, so placing a fence between your deck and the offending source will mitigate the noise. Another approach is to introduce another sound to cancel out the "noise." While a white noise machine can do this, again, it may not enhance the mood you want. The sound of moving water from waterfalls and fountains (see p. 184) is not only soothing but also can mask unwanted noise.

A deck that's separated from the house can sometimes appear to be placed randomly in the yard. To avoid this, try to anchor your deck by positioning it adjacent to a natural feature, such as a tree or rock outcropping. If this isn't possible, help create a "sense of place" for your deck by including new plantings and low fences or walls. In addition, outfit your deck with things that are meaningful to you, like artwork or other special objects.

Nestled among the trees, surrounded by lush foliage, and slightly raised above the ground like a small grey island in a green sea, this deck looks like the perfect place to shed the cares of the day. Neatly stacked between the trunks, the firewood creates a rugged, if temporary, privacy screen.

Walkways: Getting to Your Getaway Deck

Plans for a remote deck retreat should also include an easy way to get there—a walkway. In addition to the practical aspects of building a path to your deck, such as keeping your feet dry when the lawn is soaked, a walkway can help you set the mood you want to create. Walks can be a simple stepping-stone path, a narrow ribbon of pebbles, or a broad swath of brick or concrete pavers. They can be straight and direct or curved and meandering. After you've determined the location of your deck, try out different routes to it from the house and choose one that suits you best.

Home Entry

In an effort to turn modern-day houses into homes, a significant amount of attention, time, and money is spent on gourmet kitchens and large master suites. However, there's one important feature that often gets left out—home entries.

The experience of entering a house actually influences the way people feel once they're inside. If the entrance is too abrupt, there is no sense of arrival. Transitional spaces, however, provide a distinct signal to someone approaching and entering your home that says they are moving into a more private world and that they should act accordingly. Transitional spaces are also important when people leave your home, providing a place for guests to linger as they say their good-byes.

Front porches serve as transitional spaces, but their roofs, which may be difficult to integrate with your home's architecture, darken interior rooms and limit views. An entry deck might be a better fit. There are a few important elements that will help make your entry deck a success.

The first is its relationship to the front door. If possible, the floor of the deck should be level with, or no more than 6 in. to 7 in. below, the interior floor. With this arrangement, rather than being precariously perched on the top of a narrow step, your arriving guests will feel safe and focus their attention on greeting you. Alternately, a spacious top-step landing can achieve a similar effect.

Second, an entry deck should at least incorporate a small roof. Not only will it shelter guests who arrive when it's raining or snowing, but it will also serve to clearly mark the location of the front door. The entry roof should be large enough for several guests to gather under at one time. It should also be visually substantial so that it is in scale with the house and doesn't look like a tacked-on afterthought.

Finally, make your guests feel welcome as they approach your house by including a generous set of steps (see p. 156) that lead to the entry deck. Steps that are wide enough to allow people to walk side-by-side eliminate what can be a slightly awkward moment as your guests decide who should "go first."

top • There's no question about how to get into this home. The combination of stained and painted wood makes this entry deck stand out. A generous top landing and roof overhead can accommodate numerous guests with baggage in any weather.

above • Even though it's obscured by a thick bouquet of flowers, the red-brick walkway clearly indicates how to reach the front door. Once at the steps, it's a short trip up to the entry deck. The closely spaced balusters and thick posts give the deck an appropriately substantial feel.

Although relatively simple, this on-grade entry deck is the hub of comings and goings. Stone steps connect the driveway to the front door, while a stepping-stone path shows the way to the gardens. The deck continues along the side of the house, where it links up with other first-floor spaces.

Multiple Decks, Multiple Uses

Challenge encourages creativity, and that is certainly evident in the three decks that adorn the side of this modern residence. The narrow urban lot and stately tree severely restrict the horizontal possibilities, but the designer was able to meet the owner's ambitious wish list with careful space planning and effective use of vertical space. Beginning at the top, the third-floor balcony offers a cozy seating area off of the master bedroom, while, just below it, a bistro table invites the homeowners to bring their morning coffee out from the kitchen and enjoy it on the second-floor deck. An on-grade dining deck, which is paired with the outdoor patio kitchen, completes the trio. A space-saving, spiral stairway efficiently connects all three decks.

The slender steel columns and railings complement the home's architecture, while their minimalist appearance brings a sense of calm to the deck structure, which could, very easily, otherwise feel busy. The sense of calm is enhanced by the subtle grey paint and the use of the same decking material for the stair treads and the balcony's sunshade.

The view from the top of the spiral stairs reveals the overall plan of the yard and the well-thought-out relationship between the different elements. Rectangular stepping stones mimic the shape of the decks and pool, and the hot tub, like the decks, is raised above the pool.

left · The comfortable, "sink-into-me" balcony chairs are a nice counterpoint to the cool steel posts and railings, while the retractable awning allows this treetop deck to be enjoyed even when the sun is blistering hot. A sense of enclosure and a bit of privacy are created by the steel mesh that replaces the railing balusters.

below · A long section of decking creates a generous walkway that joins the upper decks and the interior rooms with the on-grade dining area and outdoor kitchen. From this angle, the spiral stairs appear to be a graceful piece of sculpture, a vertical element that's a nice counterpoint to the walkway it rises up from.

TYPES OF

A deck is a wonderful and useful addition to a home. Proper planning includes familiarizing yourself with different structural categories of decks so you can choose one that suits both your home and your outdoor living needs.

DECKS

Identifying Decks by Structure

Unlike patios, which generally must follow the contours of the land, and covered porches, which can be restricted by rooflines, decks are subject to relatively few structural constraints. This means that it's possible to add a deck to your house just about anywhere you want one. You can tuck a small deck into a corner of your house and turn that lonely corner into a peaceful getaway. Or, use a larger deck to help unify whole sections of your house.

Depending on the effect you want to achieve, a deck can blend in with its surroundings or make a bold statement. For example, railings can be made to virtually disappear or be a prominent element. Stairs can be placed discreetly out of the way or be an integral part of the deck's design.

Although decks come in a dizzying array of shapes, sizes, and styles, they can be identified by their relationship to the ground and/or home and grouped into general categories: on-grade, low-rise or tall elevated, multilevel, deck/patio and deck/porch combinations, rooftop, and balconies.

As you begin to think about the deck of your dreams, take a walk around the outside of your house and assess the lay of the land. Is the ground level and close to the first floor or is it sloping? Is there a big drop from the front to the back of your house? Are you considering building a deck off of the second floor?

Then read through the following pages and familiarize yourself with the various deck types. As you do, you will probably find houses with conditions that are similar to yours and decks that will work for your home. But also notice the differences among the various decks. Let them inspire you and be open to the possibility that a type of deck you hadn't originally considered may one day grace your home.

above · The flat roofs of city buildings just call out to be transformed with the construction of a deck. You'll be rewarded with some new space and a million dollar view.

facing page top · The formal style of this low-rise elevated deck, with its carefully detailed posts and glass panels, is carried to completion by the solid and tightly-spaced skirting.

facing page bottom · Facing the posts of this deck with the same stone used on the walls ties the deck in with the house. Had the stairs been built at 90° to the deck they would have been less visually intrusive when viewed from the basement windows and blocked less light.

On-grade

Even though the term "on-grade" suggests a deck that is constructed directly on the ground, a deck that is close enough (less than 30 in.) to the ground so that, by code, it may not be required to have a railing (see p. 148), can be considered an on-grade deck. When thinking about adding outdoor, on-grade living space, you have a choice between a deck and a patio. While both can be viable options, on-grade decks have some advantages over patios.

Some types of patios are cost-competitive with decks; however, if you want to build a deck or patio level with the floor of your house and it's about 24 in. above the ground, the price advantage can tilt in favor of decks. Additional expenses such as retaining walls, gravel fill, and extensive waterproofing can make patios much more costly.

On-grade decks are the simplest type of deck to build and are also relatively easy to add on to or modify. This means that your deck can be designed to grow in stages as your budget allows. And let's face it: Even with the best planning, we often don't account for everything. After using your deck for a while, you might discover a shortcoming or two that you'd like to correct. Of course, life has a way of springing surprises on us from time to time, but it's usually not a big problem to build on additional deck space to accommodate an unexpectedly growing family.

In areas of the country that experience freezing temperatures and snow, on-grade decks can be used when patios might not. A deck's smooth surface makes it fairly easy to clear off snow—if you have a south- or west-facing deck, the sun may do the job for you. This means you can use your deck on sunny days in the middle of winter.

above • Conveniently located right next to and at the same level as the back door, this narrow on-grade deck provides just enough room to sneak away for a quick snack or a private phone call.

above • This unique, on-grade deck gives new meaning to the phrase "bringing the outside indoors." The 2x4 decking, which is installed on edge, is bisected at the house wall by a sliding glass door, creating an interior as well as an exterior deck.

Access Hatches

If the construction of an on-grade deck will block access to utilities such as sprinkler valves or electrical connections, plan to build a hatch either in the top or side of the deck.

Virtually flush with the first floor as well as the lawn, this on-grade deck provides a seamless transition from inside to outdoors.

If one of your goals is to expand your home's sense of interior space, an on-grade deck, particularly when it's built flush with the floor, may be the better choice. Perhaps because they are constructed with materials that are similar to, or mimic, those used inside the home, on-grade decks can feel more like extensions of indoor spaces than patios.

In addition to expanding your living space, on-grade decks perform another important function—they act as a bridge, creating a transitional space between your home and the ground and tying it to the surrounding landscape. On-grade decks can also follow a gently sloping lawn, stepping down in sections to maintain contact with the ground.

above • Subtlety and simplicity are sometimes the best strategy, and that is the case with this on-grade deck. The white-painted band joist matches the house trim and siding, while the grey of the decking complements the darker roof.

Dealing with Ground Moisture

Moisture can be a problem for on-grade decks where the joists actually touch the ground, blocking the flow of air under the deck and allowing excess moisture to accumulate. In addition to creating an environment that promotes rot and decay, this moisture can enter the bottom of wooden deck boards. The decking surface, which is exposed to the sun and wind, is typically drier. This moisture imbalance can cause the deck boards to cup. To minimize this problem, put down a water vapor–retarding membrane (such as 6-mil black polyethylene sheeting) before the joists are installed. Also, plan to install vents in various locations around the perimeter of the deck.

above • The simple, backless benches built into the perimeter of this deck not only provide a place to sit or lie down, but they also act as a low railing, preventing people from making a misstep and tumbling off of the edge.

The clean, unadorned lines of this deck and the thick edge-banding are intended to match the architecture of the modern house with which it's paired. The color of the deck and the home's glass-panel walls makes it almost appear that the house is sitting right in the sand.

Elevated

If the first floor of your home is significantly higher than your yard, you will need to build an elevated deck. Although some elevated decks can literally span a long distance, any deck that is 30 in. or more above the ground can be called an elevated deck. While many elevated decks are 8 ft. to 9 ft. tall, it's not unusual, on steeply sloping sites or with second-floor decks, for decks to be 12 ft. or more in the air. When considering elevated decks, it can be helpful to break them into two groups—low-rise elevated decks (from 30 in. to 7 ft. off the ground) and tall elevated decks (7 ft. or more off the ground). Each has different but related challenges.

An elevated deck not only creates additional living space but also can provide you with an entirely new point of view by opening vistas you might not have known existed. And if, when standing in your house looking out a window, you've felt cut off from your landscape, an elevated deck, with a simple set of stairs, can easily reconnect you with your backyard.

LOW-RISE ELEVATED DECKS

When you're on a low-rise elevated deck, the experience is not too different from that of being on an on-grade deck. It's when you view the elevated deck from the ground that the differences become clear. All elevated decks reveal more of their structural components (see pp. 126–129) than their on-grade counterparts and, by default, create a certain amount of space between the bottom of the floor system and the ground. Therein lies the question: What should be done with the extra space?

If you have a low-rise elevated deck, the space underneath it can be used for different things. If it's tall enough, it can be used as a storage area (see pp. 116–117). However, unless the decking is watertight, be sure that what you store won't be ruined if it gets wet. Another common use for the space underneath a deck is to hide mechanical equipment such as pumps. Or if a hot tub or spa is part of the plans, it can be dropped into the space below the deck floor so that the top is flush with the decking.

Although structural elements are not necessarily attractive, they may not be that noticeable when a deck is only 3 ft. to 4 ft. tall, particularly if the deck floor is cantilevered beyond the posts and beams. In this case, you may decide to leave the space open. Also, some people like the look of a deck that seems to float above the ground. However, the opposite is also true. You may feel that such a deck appears unfinished and want to build a skirt around the perimeter or screen it with plants (see pp. 48-49) to hide the structural components and dark recess underneath.

TALL ELEVATED DECKS

Enclosing the underside of tall elevated decks is usually not a viable option because there's often living space— either a walkout basement or first floor—and windows below them. This means that the underside of the deck and the unattractive stamped-metal brackets and hangers will be in plain view. This is especially true if you plan to use the space underneath the deck as additional living space. If this will be a concern for you, discuss with your builder ways to mitigate the hardware's appearance, such as painting it, using custom-made hardware, or hiding it. It's also possible, particularly when creating a watertight deck, to cover everything with a ceiling.

facing page • The simple and crisp straight lines of the doors, windows, railing, skirting, and steps play well together on this rural home. The grand set of steps invites large groups up to the ample deck or the wide entrance to the indoors.

above • The straightforward, yet strong geometric shapes of this house are enlivened by the window placement and stacked shed dormers. The deck, with its fantail steps, continues the theme.

Perhaps a bigger challenge is making a tall elevated deck—or more precisely, its most prominent feature, the posts—look attractive. To avoid a random, hodgepodge appearance, try to relate the posts to the home's architectural elements, for example, by aligning them with the spaces between the doors and windows.

The size of the posts is also an issue. Even though 4x4 posts are usually physically strong enough to provide the necessary support, they are almost always visually too weak. Using 6x6 or even 8x8 posts will result in a huge improvement. Also, posts that are too far apart can appear lonely. To create more visual mass, consider using more posts than the number required by code or adding bracing, boxing, or low walls (see the drawing on the facing page). If you want to double or triple up the posts, make sure they won't get in the way of traffic flow or living space. If you add bracing, make sure it doesn't block access to the underside of the deck. Boxing adds a raised-pier look to a deck, while a low wall can be used as additional seating or as a railing, even if one isn't required by code.

Very tall elevated decks face another problem, lateral stability. To address this, tall elevated decks may need additional bracing. One effective way to achieve this bracing is by running the decking boards at a 45-degree angle to the floor joists. Other measures include installing angle braces on the posts and bracing to the joists. If you and your builder have any doubts, check with a structural engineer.

People have different feelings about height. To get a sense of what an elevated deck will feel like, you might want to visit an existing deck that is about the same height above the ground as yours will be. If you feel a little squeamish or for legitimate safety reasons, you might decide to build railings that are higher than codes require (see p. 148).

One thing to keep in mind is that tall elevated decks will shade the sun and darken the interior spaces below. To minimize this phenomenon, you can add additional windows, replace some of the decking with a grate, or create light-well openings.

top and above • **While a series of thick posts support one end of the deck, a steel beam carries the other side, eliminating the need for intermediate supports and resulting in an unobstructed view from the below-deck patio. The view from the upper deck is not too shabby either. The thin top rail is in keeping with the rest of the deck's structure, and the wire mesh that's used in lieu of balusters virtually disappears.**

Visually Enhancing Deck Posts

To avoid having your deck appear to be sitting on spindly, undersized posts, consider employing one of these options.

Diagonal Bracing

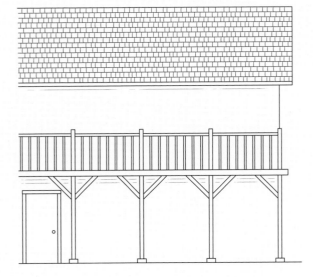

Doubling or Tripling Posts

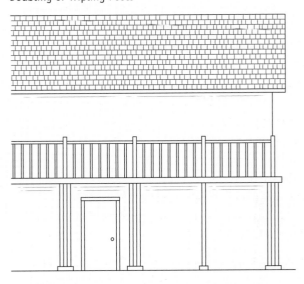

Boxing

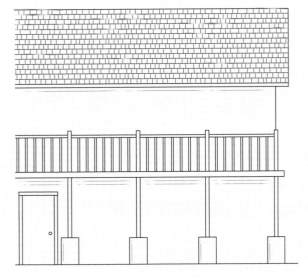

Low Wall

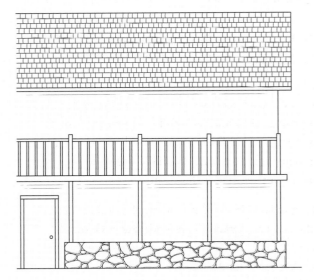

Skirting and Screening

When you first think of deck skirting, does the ubiquitous diamond-patterned latticework spring immediately to mind? If so, you need to think again because there are many options to choose from and even options yet to be designed. Instead of looking like an afterthought, skirting and screening can be an integral part of your deck that not only hides its underside from view but also enhances its style and beauty.

1. Sized to harmonize with the railing balusters and painted to match the trim, this smart-looking skirt goes beyond mere utility. It's an important and dynamic design element. 2. The small openings and narrow wooden strips of this square-patterned latticework help to reduce the impact of the skirting enclosing the tall elevated deck. The effect might have been more successful had the wood been stained a more subdued color. 3. Closely spaced and thick with foliage, the plantings near the edge of this on-grade deck screen most of the framing from view. 4. Completing a "study in white," square lattice encloses both the deck and the stairs. The neutral hue is a perfect background against which to display the soft foliage and bright colors of container plants. 5. This linear skirt is perfectly in tune with the horizontal structure of the deck's railing. Notice how the alternating widths of the skirtboards echo the rhythm of wide space/narrow space created by the metal rails.

Multilevel

A multilevel deck can be defined as any deck that incorporates a level change. Although the difference in height could range from as little as a single step to many feet, requiring one or more sets of stairs in between, the connected sections of deck should be large enough to stand on their own. On-grade, elevated, and rooftop decks can all be connected to create a multilevel deck and serve as an exterior route to two or more floors in a home. You could say that multilevel decks suffer from split personalities, but their unique quality serves some important functions.

Very large decks can be physically imposing, particularly when viewed from the ground. A multilevel deck reduces its visual mass, keeping it at an appropriate scale. Small level changes are also an effective way to add visual interest to what otherwise would be a monolithic deck. However, to avoid having it feel arbitrary, it's important to relate the change in height to an architectural feature, such as the corner of a building or a set of steps that goes to the ground. Level changes of 6 in. or so (one step) can be hard to distinguish, particularly in dim light. To make them easier to see, consider changing the direction of the decking or create a "landing zone" with a different decking pattern or another decking material.

Another reason to build a multilevel deck is to preserve or enhance a view from either the deck or house. On a very deep deck, unless the furniture is placed close to the railing, downhill views can be at least partially blocked by the deck or obscured by the railing. And the same is true when inside the house—a deep deck will probably cut off a significant amount of what was once a beautiful vista. In both cases, stepping the deck down several feet can help to maintain the views.

Changing levels is an effective way to differentiate spaces and create deck "rooms." For example, the main level might be the cooking and dining area, a level down perhaps the sitting area, and yet another level, either up or down from the lounge area, set aside for a hot tub.

Sun, shade, view, privacy—this relatively small, multilevel deck makes the most of tight quarters. The upper deck, blessed with sun and an unobstructed view, is accessed off a bedroom yet conveniently connected to the lower deck by a straight-run set of stairs, which continues down to the ground. Screened by trees, you can enjoy lunch on the lower deck or slip around the corner and read a book in the shade.

left • To help preserve the view and to afford some measure of privacy, this hot-tub deck is almost a full flight of steps lower than the upper decks. The lower deck also connects to the on-grade patio, but because it's a couple of steps above the patio, it maintains the feeling of being a separate space.

below • This expansive bilevel deck is designed to accommodate large gatherings while preserving the view from the bank of French doors. A narrow deck just outside the doors leads to the upper dining deck, which is positioned off to the right and out of the line of sight. A set of broad stairs, punctuated with tiered planters, connects the deep, lounging deck, positioning it below the view.

A Family-Friendly Design

The existing south-facing deck on this one-story home boasted a great, sunny exposure but little else. The wooden decking had been neglected and was beginning to throw up splinters. Although the deck's overall footprint was reasonably sized, its original two-level design severely reduced the effective usable area, making the deck "live" small, too small for the couple's growing family. And, the lack of any overhead protection limited the amount of time that it was comfortable to be on the deck.

The solution was to completely remove the existing deck, start fresh, and create a family-friendly, multilevel outdoor space. A new, full-service kitchen now occupies much of the area of the original upper deck, and on the same level, a comfortable dining "room" extends beyond the house walls to capture the surrounding views. A large pergola shelters and helps define both spaces. Turned at a 45-degree angle and down a short flight of steps, the open-to-the-sky hot-tub deck is out of the direct line of sight—yet, for safety's sake, it's still within view. Stairs leading down from this second deck to the yard anticipate phase two of the project, a walkway and patio.

above • The small but efficient L-shaped kitchen is tucked up against the house, leaving much of the upper deck unobstructed.

left • The change in level creates a separate "room" for the hot tub that's close to, yet feels far removed from, the activities of the upper deck.

Generously proportioned, the dining area provides lots of circulation room. The high stools can be used by those who want to offer encouragement to the cook or be the first ones served.

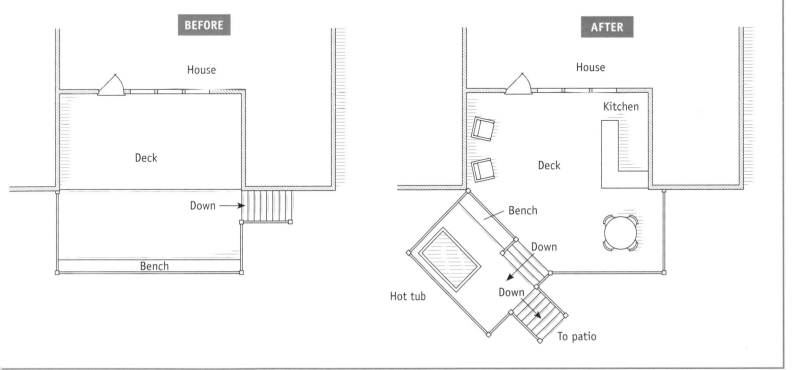

BEFORE

House

Deck

Down →

Bench

AFTER

House

Kitchen

Deck

Bench

Down

Down

Hot tub

Down

To patio

Combination

While looking for ways to make better use of their yards and landscape and to accommodate the ever-expanding list of outdoor activities, some homeowners are building patios and porches in combination with their decks. Of course, it's probably not a good idea to build a deck/patio/porch combination just because your neighbor does. Take a hard look at your lifestyle, and your budget, to determine if such a combination is a good fit for you. Also, your home's architecture or landscape may limit your options. However, in the right situation, deck combinations can enhance your outdoor time.

DECK AND PATIO COMBINATIONS

A patio can be the perfect companion for an on-grade or low-rise elevated deck, as this combination provides expanded design options. For example, if there's a place to dine on the patio as well as the deck, you can eat your everyday meals on the deck, closer to the house, and use the patio dining space for larger or more formal gatherings. If you have your heart set on stone countertops and a masonry grill, putting your outdoor kitchen on the patio rather than the deck may make more sense.

Making a deck and patio combination work well requires planning. Of critical importance is the connection between the two. People must be able to move freely and easily from one area to the other. This means that a narrow, standard-width stair of 3 ft. just won't do. Stairs should be a minimum of 4 ft. wide; 5-ft.- or 6-ft.-wide steps are even better. This will allow people to pass each other coming and going, even if they are carrying a tray full of food. A strong visual connection can also help join a deck to the patio. Proper orientation and open-style railings will allow the folks on the deck to see and talk with those on the patio and vice versa.

above • Taking advantage of the relative ease with which stone pavers can be shaped into curves, this patio's flowing edge is a nice counterpoint to the deck's intersecting, rectangular forms. The curve is also functional and creates a seating "alcove."

above • Just as a blue shirt can bring out the color of blue eyes, this deck, painted to match the house, accentuates the blue of this patio's stone.

Coordinating Decking and Patio Materials

In addition to designing an efficient flow from your deck to your patio, you should give some thought to their visual integration. When choosing decking and patio materials, there are three important elements of style to keep in mind—pattern, texture, and color. Because there are fewer options for decking than patio surfacing materials, begin by selecting the decking (pp. 132–145), then choose the patio materials.

Whether you choose a simple or intricate decking pattern, you need to decide whether you want the patio to mimic it or contrast with it. For example, if your decking boards will run parallel to the house with no change in direction, you may want to spice things up a bit and install the patio materials in a more interesting pattern, such as herringbone. And the reverse is true. If you choose an intricate decking pattern, you might consider a simple pattern for the patio.

All decking has a relatively smooth and even surface. Stone and masonry used to surface patios have rougher textures, and there are differences among them. Machine-cut, finished stone, such as bluestone, is much smoother than blasted stone that is hand split on-site. Concrete and brick pavers can be finished with various surface textures, and poured concrete can be troweled smooth or stamped with an array of available patterns. You can decide if you want to have a smooth-surfaced patio that's similar to your decking or a rougher one that adds some punch.

The same is true when thinking about color coordination. Decking and patio materials are available in a number of colors, and you can choose colors that blend or contrast with each other. It can be useful to take a trip to the local masonry-supply yard to take a look at some samples. Keep in mind that the color shades of most stone and masonry vary from quarry to quarry and batch to batch, so the sample colors most likely will not be an exact match to what's delivered to your door.

above • The decking pattern, a straightforward "running bond," and the grey color of the stone pavers blend perfectly with the on-grade deck. With its simple curve, the plant-lined walkway completes the understated arrangement.

above • A deck and patio combination was a practical choice for connecting this home to the backyard on a sloping site.

right • When we hear the words "great view" we often think of sweeping panoramas. As the view from this deck demonstrates, close-in vignettes can be just as satisfying.

right • By surrounding small, rectangular sections of boards with borders, this decking echos the shapes of the bluestone patio.

A Perfectly Paired Deck and Patio

This house previously had a small stoop and shallow, steep steps stuck onto the back. They were not only totally inadequate but also posed a safety risk. Snow and ice collected on them during the winter, and walking up and down the steps was dangerous for the owners' short-legged dogs and aging parents during all seasons. To remedy both problems, the owners built a covered deck where they can sit and watch the morning sunrise. It steps effortlessly down to a patio.

The patio provides a place to cook, additional seating, and a raised fire pit for cozying up to during the cool swing seasons. The concrete patio was stained to match the deck, unifying the two, and the native grasses and stones add a serene, desertlike quality, which has become an important part of the owners'—and neighbors'—view.

BEFORE

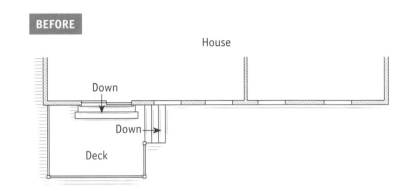

The homeowners realized that when sitting inside their house the ceiling of the deck cover would figure prominently in their view. So, rather than using an inexpensive material, such as painted plywood, they decided to go with a more costly option—clear-finished V-jointed pine. The washed stone below the deck eliminates grass-cutting and weed-pulling maintenance and ties in with the overall scheme.

This deck and patio combination is a good example of how a number of different materials can be used without the overall look becoming too busy. The house, brick pillars, concrete, concrete pavers used to top the fire pit, and even most of the native stone all share a similar color tone that helps to tie everything together. The fluid patio connects all the components.

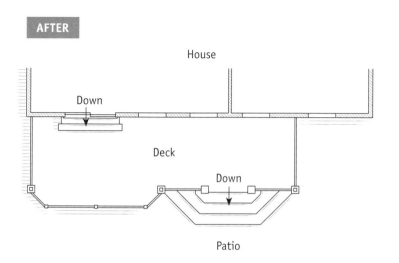

AFTER

House

Down

Deck

Down

Patio

DECK AND PORCH COMBINATIONS

Another popular approach is to combine decks with screened porches. In many areas of the country, during certain times of the year or as night approaches, biting and buzzing insects can make sitting on an open deck an unpleasant experience. Screening in a section of a deck is a great solution to this problem— you are protected from the offending marauders yet still able to enjoy being outdoors.

Whether it's to escape the scorching sun or a quick summer cloudburst, there are times when you just want a solid roof over your head. Incorporating a covered deck or open porch with your deck will give you the flexibility to enjoy your deck when the climate is less than perfect. Without the walls associated with screened porches, these spaces can flow together seamlessly.

The door to this screened porch is appropriately positioned in a corner and directly opposite the flight of stairs. This keeps the main line of travel out of the way, allowing maximum use of the companion deck.

Covered Decks vs. Porches

What is the difference between a porch and a covered deck? The answer might surprise you. Like many things, the answer is subjective and based upon which part of the country a person is from. For many people, almost any outdoor structure that has a roof on it is considered to be a porch, but for others the distinction lies with where the deck or porch is located and the type of materials and construction techniques that are used to build it. As an example, in certain areas of the West, porches are on the front of the house and are generally small and made of concrete—what some might call a stoop. Decks are in the rear of the house and built with wood-framed construction and decking boards that are spaced apart. The fact that it may or may not have a roof, or cover, is simply a matter of personal taste or whether one is required by the elements—it's just another feature people may choose to add to their deck.

left and below • Given the opportunity to take advantage of a drop-dead gorgeous backyard view, it's not surprising that decks and screened porches are an integral part of this home's design. Biting insects, no doubt, come with the bucolic setting so, appropriately, most of the square footage is allotted to the porches. The smaller decks, used primarily for sitting, are connected to each other by a narrow walkway that fronts the larger screened porch. A generous, double-sided set of steps leads to the lawn. The steps can double as seating or plant stands.

Rooftop

A rooftop deck doesn't actually have to be on top of the roof of your home. While it's certainly possible to build such a deck, the pitched roofs that cover most houses make that more difficult. It's usually more feasible to build rooftop decks on structures that can be constructed with, or converted to have, flat roofs. Covered porches, garages, small additions, and bump-outs such as bay windows are all possible candidates for a rooftop deck.

Building a rooftop deck requires coordination with the house floor plan. Perhaps the major challenge is access—exactly how are you going to get onto it? Even if you're planning a rooftop deck in conjunction with a new lower deck and roofed porch, it's unlikely that there will be an exterior door in just the right spot. You'll have to install one. However, before you add a door in your master bedroom, be sure you're ready to put up with the extra traffic that new deck will surely attract.

Another access issue you may confront when adding a rooftop deck to an existing structure is floor height. It's possible that the floor of your house and your new rooftop deck will be uneven. It's not much of a problem if the deck is lower; you just connect the two with some steps. However, when the deck is higher, it's more of a challenge. You can build a step or two inside the house to get to the proper height, but any more than that and you may run out of room to install a door. Another approach you can take to create space for exterior steps is to lower a small portion of the roof that will support the deck, but this might not always be possible. Constructing the deck to as low a profile as possible (for example, by using narrower joists) can also help.

Waterproofing the roof underneath the deck is also important, especially when the area below is finished, interior space. Extra money spent on making sure the roofing material, installation methods, and detailing are the highest quality you can afford will pay dividends for years to come.

above · Building this garage with a flat roof not only allowed light-admitting French doors to be installed in the room behind it but also offered the perfect place to construct a rooftop deck. The garage overhang is detailed to match the house trim and conceals a gutter that delivers the rain runoff to the downspout.

right and below • There's nothing like a rooftop deck to make city living feel more civil. The arched arbor and flanking flower boxes mark the gateway to this urban oasis. The unique parquet decking panels that form the floor are supported on individually adjustable plastic pedestals. The pedestals eliminate the need for floor joists and easily conform to the minor irregularities in the roof's surface.

Balconies

It seems that Romeo and Juliet have forever infused balconies with a sense of romance, and it's easy to see why. Their small size and location—usually off of a bedroom—make them intimate. Although they could be considered elevated decks, balconies are different in the way they're constructed. Unlike elevated decks, balconies are not supported by posts that go down to the ground but rather are held up by cantilevers or brackets.

A cantilever is an unsupported section of floor, which, in residential construction, is achieved by extending the home's floor joists beyond the plane of the exterior wall. As a result, a cantilevered balcony appears to float in the air. Assuming that the joists run in the proper direction, cantilevers are relatively easy to build in new construction, but they can be difficult to add on to an existing structure. To do so requires opening up the interior ceiling and installing new, longer joists next to the existing ones. Even if it's possible, this approach significantly adds to the construction costs. A more reasonable approach is to support the balcony with brackets.

Brackets typically extend at a 45-degree angle from the house's exterior wall up to the outside edge of the balcony. Brackets can be simple and straight or curved and highly detailed and are made out of wood or metal. Because balcony brackets put additional stress on the walls, the walls may need to be reinforced.

The structural limitations of cantilevers and brackets account for the shallow depth of balconies, typically 4 ft. to 6 ft. Outfitting balconies with furniture can be a challenge. While there may be enough room for a bistro table and a couple of chairs, space for lounge chairs can be scarce. Making the balcony wider is usually not a problem, so increasing the width will enable you to position a chaise lounge or two parallel with the house.

above • **The elongated brackets beneath this narrow deck, which connects two second-floor spaces, add a bit of whimsy to the straightforward design.**

above • Even a small balcony can have a big impact. This chair-sized example provides a commanding view over the water and up the driveway. The white-painted joists, juxtaposed against the yellows of the house, give the structure additional visual weight.

left • Supported on wooden brackets, this generous second-floor balcony spans the width of the room it's attached to and shelters the door below. A similarly styled roof shades the door leading out to the balcony and allows the view to be enjoyed even during a light rain.

Growing Up, Looking Out

The owners of this 200-year-old, two-bedroom house loved their home and its magnificent location mere feet from a tidal river, but they needed more space. They hired an architect with considerable experience remodeling older homes and he faced several challenges. With this house hemmed in by the street on the front, the river at the rear, and lot restrictions on both sides, the only way to create new space was to go up. However, adding a full third floor would have overwhelmed the house and put the new peak above the height allowed by local zoning. The architect designed a gambrel-style roof, which maintained the original eave line and kept the ridge low, solving both problems while at the same time providing plenty of headroom for the new master bedroom suite it enclosed.

The first-floor living room and second-floor family room share not only the view but also the same structure—the roof that shelters the porch and forms the floor for the second-floor deck. Luckily, this roof suffered only from cosmetic deterioration and was structurally sound. Not only did local codes prohibit enlarging it, but without acquiring the requisite variances, they also might have prohibited replacing it within the same footprint. Newly detailed, the railing and trim are in keeping with, and enhance the home's historic architecture.

above · The cozy balcony is blessed with a sweeping and spectacular view of the mouth of the river and ocean beyond. French doors provide easy access to the deck and invite the view and sea breezes into the new master bedroom.

left · The porch, second-floor deck, and viewing balcony help to turn the focus of the house outward toward its most important asset—the view. Latticework on the sides of the second-floor deck railing create a measure of privacy, and the delicate lines of the cantilevered balcony are appropriately scaled for its diminutive size.

PLANNING

Although you've made some progress, there are a lot of details to attend to before your deck becomes a reality. Proper planning will help you account for them and ensure that your deck meets, or exceeds, your expectations.

YOUR DECK

The Importance of Planning

Planning is a vital step that can make or break a deck. Even a relatively modest construction project is an investment, so you want to make sure that you plan your deck's location, size, and shape to suit your home and lifestyle and add permanent accoutrements like built-ins and lighting in the proper locations to maximize the use of your outdoor living space.

Planning doesn't necessarily mean designing, although if you'd like to take a crack at it, by all means, go ahead (see the sidebar p. 73). Even if you want to try your hand at designing your deck, you should probably seek the help of a professional—either a builder or designer (see the sidebar below). He or she can help you avoid pitfalls and suggest options you might not be aware of. Proper planning requires thinking about the big picture, the entire scope of your project, so that during the design process nothing gets overlooked. Taking the time to adequately plan your project is a wise investment and accomplishes several things. It helps you avoid missteps and delays, gives you the time to incorporate special features and shop for bargains, and lets you set and stay within a budget.

In chapter 1, you gathered a lot of personal information and envisioned your dream deck. But your deck is going to be constructed in the real world, and there are a lot of unavoidable factors that will hold sway over your wishes. Taking those things into account now will minimize the surprises that might spring up later.

Assembling Your Team

A deck may seem to be a straightforward construction project, but things are not always as simple as they seem, so you may need or want to seek the services of more than one professional.

- **An architect or building designer** can assist with the design of your deck, particularly if it's complicated or large. A licensed architect is highly educated, trained, and familiar with all aspects of design and construction. Choose an architect who specializes in residential design. Building designers and interior designers usually have some amount of formal training or may belong to a professional organization that requires a minimum level of expertise. All qualified designers can prepare the plans and specifications you may need to gather prices for your project. Architects and designers typically work by the hour or charge their fee as a percentage of the cost of construction. Some states may mandate the services of a licensed architect.
- **A licensed structural engineer** may be required if your deck will be elevated or constructed on recently disturbed or unstable soils, or if you live in an area prone to earthquakes.

- **A general contractor (GC)**, often referred to as a **builder**, prepares a complete price, or estimate, for the entire scope of the work and oversees the construction of your project. A general contractor typically has employees who perform most of the work—installing the concrete piers and doing the rough and finish carpentry. However, on more involved projects, the general contractor gathers prices from and retains the services of subcontractors, such as electricians (to install lighting), plumbers/gas fitters (to install sinks and gas lines), and excavators. The GC supervises the work, coordinates the subs, and is ultimately responsible for the quality of the job. Many builders have in-house design services, and a growing number of builders specialize in building decks and porches. Of course, as a part of interviewing all builders, you should ask for a list of references and follow up by contacting them. If it's required by your state, make sure that a builder is licensed, ask to see proof of his liability insurance, and check out his reputation with the Better Business Bureau or perhaps an online review service such as Angie's List.

Although the views
of the nearby pond
and wetlands are
certainly nice
from this lower
deck, shifting the
viewpoint, as with
the balcony above,
usually offers
a different and
sometimes dramatic
perspective.

71

right • Although there's a lot going on here—a pergola with braced posts, deck railing, picket fence, little privacy fence, and skirting, the white paint ties them all together so that it doesn't look too busy.

right • This wide deck looks well-dressed with stairs that virtually span it entirely. Container plants give the steps a visual "railing" and add a punch of color to the neutral tones of the house.

below • Although decks and porches are similar, the experience of sitting on a deck that's unfettered by walls and open to the sky is definitely different than sitting on a covered porch. The outdoors is that much closer and the environment is more impactful. Here, both the porch and the deck are on grade, but the exposed deck has a rain drain built in to keep water from pooling up and damaging the wood.

The Design Process

As you think about and plan your deck, you might want to take a crack at actually creating the design. It's simply a matter of gathering some important information and approaching the process in a logical, step-by-step manner. You can use one of the many deck-design computer programs as a drawing aid, or simply use graph paper that is ruled with ¼-in. squares. By having each square represent 1 ft., you'll create ¼-in.-scale plans. At the end of this process, you will have a serviceable drawing—one, at the very least, that helps communicate your desires to designers or builders.

1. Measure the portion of your house where you plan to put the deck, and draw an "existing conditions" plan. Be sure to include the doors, windows, and other features such as chimneys and hose bibs. If you know the location of underground wires and pipes, include them, too.

2. On the existing conditions plan, note the compass reading (N, S, E, and W), solar exposure, direction of cooling summer breezes and nasty winter winds, natural features you'd like to highlight, and views you'd like to capture and/or screen out.

3. As you begin your design, look at the big picture first—the general location, size, and shape—before attending to the details of style.

4. Although it's an easy trap to fall into, don't settle on your first design, but rather try out a number of options and variations. Play with the size, shape, and orientation. One good way to do this is to lay tracing paper over the existing conditions plan and work freehand with felt-tipped pens or markers. Even if you end up choosing your initial plan, this exploration will probably enrich the end result.

5. Finally, refine the rough plan that you've chosen. Using the graph paper and ruler or drawing triangle as a guide, draw the deck's exact size and shape, locate the stairs and railings, then add additional features like built-ins and lighting.

Selecting a Location

Once you've settled on how you plan to use your deck and the type of deck you want, the next task is to determine where it should be located. As discussed in chapter 1, the major deciding factor in deck placement is usually its relationship to the interior rooms. However, several other issues—such as access, views, privacy, and the elements—can also influence your deck's placement and design. As you work through the planning process, don't be surprised if there's no perfect solution. You'll probably have to make some compromises and arrive at a location that strikes the best balance.

above right • With apparently nothing but a tangle of grass and the tall, whispering pines for company, this private deck is the perfect place to contemplate your inner thoughts or take in the peek-a-boo view of the nearby lake.

right • Appropriately sized to fit the scale of the house, this on-grade deck makes the most of its limited space. Easily accessed by a generous set of doors and situated only several inches below the first floor, the seating area is located off to the side, where it is not impacted by comings and goings.

Located in a secluded corner, this furniture grouping is arranged to encourage casual conversation. The low railing adds to the cozy feel and, during lulls in the conversation, folks can let their gaze wander over and past the nearby flowers.

ACCESS AND TRAFFIC FLOW

Don't assume that "if you build it, they will come." In the extreme, it's obvious that you will not build a deck that you can't get to. However, there are some subtler issues to be on the lookout for that can cause problems if they're ignored.

To make sure your deck isn't something that's looked at from your house more often than it's actually used, strive to make access to it as welcoming and as easy as possible. For example, if the existing door that will open up on the deck is relatively narrow, consider replacing it with one that's at least 3 ft. wide. Or better yet, install a 6-ft.-wide French or sliding door. Sometimes easy access requires more drastic measures, that is, cutting in a new door where there wasn't one.

Another way to make your deck more inviting from the inside is to build it so that the decking is on the same level as the interior floor. This approach does a better job of visually extending the inside to the outdoors, and it also eliminates the psychological barrier that a step or two can present. Although it takes some thought and well-executed construction details to deal with rainwater and snow, the first time you carry a tray full of drinks out to your deck you'll appreciate the seamless transition from inside to outside.

Closely related to access is traffic flow—the movement of your family and guests onto, within, and off of your deck. One way to plan for traffic flow is to think of it as a river with small tributaries. For example, the main "river" might be the line of travel from the house door, through the deck, and down the stairs to the lawn. The functional parts of the deck—seating, dining, and cooking areas—are best located off to the side, out of the current but easily reached. Of course, the location of the stairs plays a crucial role in controlling traffic flow.

You also need to plan for the effect this new traffic flow will have on the interior spaces of your house, particularly if you will add a new door or windows. If your deck will be a part of a larger project (for example, a kitchen remodel or addition), make sure to integrate the two. If the deck will not be part of the initial construction, plan for future traffic flow by creating a master plan that designates the location and lays out the shape of the deck.

Efficient Traffic Flow

This deck was part of a major renovation of an old farmhouse, which also included master bedroom and screened porch additions. Located between two additions and the existing house, the deck is easy to access from all three spaces, but careful attention was paid to traffic flow to make sure that access to activity areas on the deck functioned well. The primary traffic path is from the dining room door, across the deck, and down the steps to the lawn. People coming from the screened porch and bedroom create second and third lines of travel. Locating these doors opposite each other and closer to the house wall keeps this "hallway" compact, forming a T as the primary path and allowing for efficient use of activity space.

During mealtime, the chef uses the travel space behind the grill and adjacent countertop and service bar, which affords plenty of room for cooking and serving. The stairs are positioned slightly, and purposefully, off-center to allot more space to the large seating area and a bit less to the dining area. When there are a lot of guests for dinner, an additional table can be set up and spill over into the main traffic path.

above · Wide doors make it easy to see the deck beyond, and they make getting onto a deck effortless. Set up in a corner of the deck, the dining table is out of the flow of traffic, yet still close enough to the house so that bringing out the food doesn't feel like a chore.

facing page · Thin metal furniture doesn't take up much room, thus it allows for better traffic flow around it. This deck is rather large to begin with, but this idea could make a world of difference on a smaller deck.

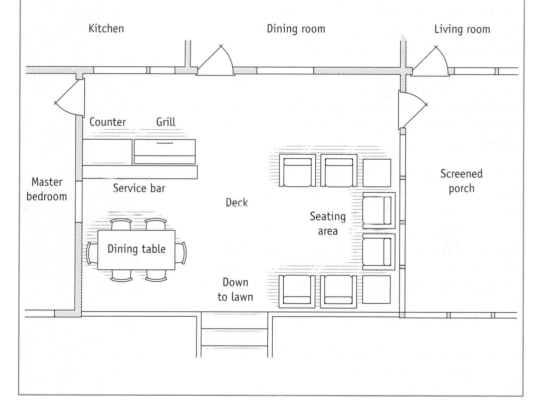

Types of Doors

If your deck plans call for replacing an existing door or adding a new one, there are a wide range of styles and materials available to fit every taste and budget. Be sure to choose one that's compatible with the style of your house. And because this door will be used frequently, choose the highest-quality door you can afford.

STEEL DOORS
$

- Come primed, ready to paint
- May rust or dent
- May not blend well with style of house or deck

SLIDING GLASS DOORS
$$–$$$

- Made with various materials
- Available with full-length, one-piece glass; true or simulated divided lights; frosted or stained glass
- Bypass-type door opening doesn't interfere with furniture

FIBERGLASS DOORS—SMOOTH AND WOOD TEXTURED
$$–$$$

- Available in various styles
- Will not rust or dent
- Can be painted or stained
- Textured-surface types can cost as much as solid-wood doors

SINGLE-SWING SOLID-WOOD PANEL DOORS
$$$

- Available in hardwoods or softwoods
- Natural beauty of wood when clear finished or stained
- Swell and shrink with changes in humidity
- Wide range of panel styles and glass sizes

FRENCH DOORS
$$$

- Made with various materials
- Available with full-length, one-piece glass; true or simulated divided lights; frosted or stained glass
- Available in styles in which both doors can open
- Door swings may get in the way

Panel

Molded

Flush

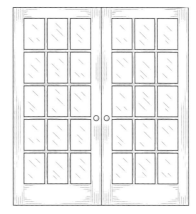

French doors

Sliding glass doors

Multiple points of access from inside the house and the yard can present an organizational challenge. The furniture placement on this deck successfully works with rather than "fights" the flow of traffic.

above · This double-swing French door unites the inside with the deck, making it feel like an extension of the interior of the home. The stairs to the lawn are off to one side but aligned with the deck's "hallway" that runs along the railing, carving out space near the brick wall for ample seating.

right · Because the backyard is fairly small, a long and shallow deck contoured along the house works best for this home. This deck is an example of how, with proper planning, a small deck can be an accessible deck.

New Doors of Opportunity

When this 1960s Colonial underwent a major renovation, the homeowners made sure that the use of and access to their backyard was not overlooked. The miniscule concrete stoop and associated concrete patio were common features for homes of that era, but they didn't fit at all with the family's lifestyle. They wanted a space that they could get to easily and connected them to the yard. Compounding the problem were two doors located so close to each other that they literally got in each other's way.

The plans called for replacing the patio with a modest, on-grade deck. As a part of the renovation, the old doors were removed, relocated, and replaced with divided-light French doors. Not only do they bring light into the house and open up views to the yard, but they also make getting to the new deck a snap.

BEFORE

below • The dining table is appropriately located in a line-of-travel dead spot. Steps down to the yard make up about three-quarters of the deck's perimeter. They successfully connect the deck and, in turn, the house to the yard and provide ample, impromptu seating.

All-Access Deck

When the homeowners needed to replace a failing deck, they also wanted to enhance the quality of the time that they spent outdoors. The upper portion of the original two-level deck wasn't wide enough to feel comfortable, while the lower section was too short. A gate and a narrow set of stairs, which severely restricted access to the backyard, further revealed the old deck's inadequate and unimaginative design.

The new deck is both wider and longer, with ample space for hanging out and enjoying the cool of the evening. One entire side of the upper deck sports a deep set of steps, which not only opens to the yard but also fans out to a walkway that leads around the house. The lower deck, which is used for dining, is bumped out at three corners for additional seating. A bump-out for the grill allows it to be close by but out of the way.

This deck design also allowed the homeowners to arrange their furniture for better traffic flow. The lounge area is located at the upper deck, so guests are instantly welcomed into a relaxing environment, while the much more active cooking and dining occurs on the lower level. This arrangement promotes a graceful transition to the party. Also, with the cooking and dining area out of the way, smoke doesn't billow into the faces of oncoming guests and guests don't walk behind the busy chef or into the personal space of those eating the meal.

BEFORE

right • Instead of ending abruptly at the edge of the house, the new steps extend beyond the corner, embracing it and reaching out into the planting bed. The 45-degree corner is carefully centered on the walkway.

The seating group is tucked into the corner, taking advantage of the shelter afforded by the house walls, while the more boisterous activity of the dining area is open to the sun, view, and breeze on all sides.

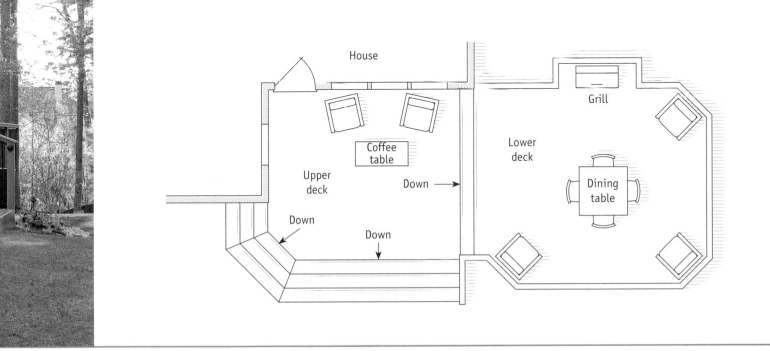

House

Grill

Coffee table

Upper deck

Down →

Lower deck

Dining table

Down

Down

VIEW

A major motivation for building a deck is for the views that are possible when there are no solid walls surrounding you and no roof overhead. Not surprisingly, trying to capture, or screen out, specific views will influence the location of your deck.

As you plan your deck, investigate potential views by standing, using a ladder if need be, in the different places you are considering locating the deck. Keep in mind that moving your position even slightly might translate into a big improvement or significant worsening of your view, so you might want to shift your deck accordingly. If the land slopes away from your deck, think about stepping it down so that the view is available from the back as well as the front of the deck.

Railings (pp. 148–155) won't obstruct the view if you're standing, but when you sit down, it's a different matter. To keep the view as open as possible, choose visually lightweight balusters, and pay particular attention to the top rail. When reclining in a lounge chair, the top rail might be right at eye level and can be annoying.

In addition to thinking about the view from the deck, consider how the deck will affect the view from your house. Again, stepping down the deck and choosing an appropriate railing system can help maintain an existing view. Or, of course, you can add additional windows or increase the size of existing ones so that you can capture the same view that the deck enjoys from the house. Keep in mind that there may be sections of the deck—such as the grilling or hot tub areas—that you don't want to see from the house or at least from a particular space, such as the living room.

The narrow top rail and thin, coated-wire infill perfectly reflect the architecture of this modern home, and their minimal profiles don't obstruct the gorgeous view of the city below.

above · Large decks can block desired views. Wanting to avoid this, the designer of this deck lowered some of the outer sections. To take advantage of their natural shade, a few of the trees were incorporated into the deck.

left · The lines of sight to the sky are clear, but given how close this chair is to the railing, the wide-board top rail may negatively impact the other views by blocking those that are straight ahead and being annoyingly within one's peripheral vision when looking downward.

A Deck with a Panoramic View

When your house is surrounded by trees, why not take advantage of the privacy they provide and surround your house with a deck? That's exactly what the owners of this tucked-in-the-woods home did. Numerous windows look onto this spacious deck, which encompasses three sides of the house and offers ready access from the house through any of the many doors, making it easy for folks to take advantage of the forest-like views. The naturally finished wood decking and top rails pay homage to the neighboring trees, and the substantial posts echo the tree trunks. Round metal balusters cleverly replace what would typically be wooden ones, whose thick cross sections would have been visually heavy and obtrusive.

above right • This set of steps leads to a stone landing and stone steps, which, in turn, lead to an under-deck patio that's outside the lower level. The roughsawn treads combine well with the textured stone.

right • A small entry deck and short flight of stairs connect a wing of the house that's a half-level higher than the main house to the deck. The thick, open-riser stair treads are in keeping with the heavy-wood theme and meet building code requirements for the maximum space allowed between treads.

To eliminate unnecessary space, the corners of the deck are cut at a 45-degree angle. Here, two large ceramic pots mark the angle's intersection and create a sense of place for a simple bench.

The wide wooden frame of this gate might be difficult to open and could sag over time. To eliminate those potential problems, a castor wheel was installed near the free end for support.

This intricately styled bench sits opposite the other cut corner, which is also flanked by pots. The relatively long distance between the bench and the railing ensures that the wide top rail will not interfere with the view of the woods from the bench.

PRIVACY

If some or all of your deck will be in sight of your neighbors or a street, you might want to find ways to create some privacy. First, determine how intrusive the offending line of sight might be—is it close to or far away from your deck? Then, to decide on the most effective remedy, determine the direction of the line of sight—is the view onto your deck coming from below, straight on, or above? Views from below are easily screened with solid railings or low walls, which will shield you from sight when you're sitting on your deck. The same may be true for straight-on lines of sight, but views from above are the most difficult to screen out. They may require tall walls and perhaps some sort of overhead structure, like a pergola.

above · Tucked up close to the house and shielded from outside by the dense foliage, this deck has the feel of a quiet refuge. It, of course, takes time for plants to get this mature, so newly installed privacy landscaping might need an assist from a temporary screen or fence.

left · Privacy is sometimes a matter of degrees. Even in situations that, at first, feel exposed, some measure of seclusion can be attained by locating a deck out of the direct line of sight of windows and line of travel generated by doors.

facing page · Although the thicket of tropical plants certainly sets the stage, it's the low-key color scheme and harmonious shapes that make the mood for this tranquil scene. The muted greys are perked up, just a bit, by the blue of the cushions, and the circular fountain, end table, and fire pit have a centering effect.

Privacy Screening

Even though one of the major reasons for building a deck is to be "open" to the great outdoors, there are situations that call for a little privacy or protection, and every situation is different. So carefully analyze what you're trying to accomplish with your screening, and choose a structure or method accordingly.

1. This arch-topped solid wall looks like an extension of the contiguous house wall, but at three-quarter height, it does its job of blocking the line of site to the chair from the neighbors without feeling overbearing. 2. Leaving small spaces between wide boards allows breezes to slip through without compromising the desired privacy because, at a distance, it's virtually impossible to actually make out anything through the cracks. Finishing the top of a heavy privacy screen with something that's visually lighter makes it feel less imposing. 3. Solid walls are often necessary to block out sound and create privacy in densely packed neighborhoods; however, they can make people feel claustrophobic. The vines covering these brick and wood walls create a feeling of sitting in a secluded glen rather than a walled-off encampment. 4. When viewed from the ground below, this tall privacy screen could have felt overbearing, but the use of small horizontal and vertical members lessens its impact. 5. The widely spaced lattice that forms the upper portion of this two-tier privacy screen isn't obtrusive and affords people the opportunity to enjoy the adjacent courtyard as they walk onto or off of the deck. 6. From the posts' pedestal bases to the sculpted shapes of the pergola above, this finely crafted privacy screen does its job with panache. The vertical members on the side are bolstered by horizontal pieces behind, which combine to screen out the view.

PROTECTION FROM THE ELEMENTS

Without the protection provided by a solid roof and walls, decks are open to the effects and subject to the whims of weather. For the most part, this is a good thing, and it's why we love decks so much. But without proper planning, this positive attribute can turn into a negative.

The **sun** is arguably the most influential of all the elements. Depending on where you live, its warming rays can be welcome in the spring and fall but can be searing in the middle of summer. The sun travels across the sky from east to west and is low in the sky in the morning and evening and reaches its highest point at noon. Take into account the sun's location at different times of the day as you think about the location of your deck.

East-facing decks get the sun first, so they are often a desirable place for that morning coffee in the summer, but they can be a bit cool in the evenings in the early spring and late fall. South-facing decks receive the sun all day long. In the summer, when it's high in the sky, the sun can make a deck uncomfortably hot. Overhead structures (see pp. 95–97), like pergolas and awnings, can provide cooling shade and shelter. West-facing decks are wonderful gathering places where you can enjoy colorful sunsets and warming rays on chilly spring and fall afternoons. However, on hot days the low western sun can be difficult to screen, forcing people to retreat to other parts of the deck or even inside. If it's possible, position your deck to take advantage of the shade offered by nearby trees or provide some type of movable shading.

above · This skylight answers the question: How can you construct a waterproof covering over your deck without blocking the light? When left near the edge, the table and chairs can enjoy direct sunshine, and when it rains, they can be quickly pulled back under cover.

facing page · The amount, intensity, and direction of the sun that strikes a deck heavily influence a pergola's design. When more shade is desired, the purlins, the smaller pieces of wood that are attached to the rafters, are installed closer together.

Microclimates

Although broad generalizations can be made about the North American climate, areas that are geographically close—even building lots that are side by side—can experience very different weather conditions. Trees, walls, hills, hollows, and even the position of your home on its lot affect the climate of any area of your yard, creating microclimates. Keep these microclimates in mind as you plan your deck.

Sun and Shade through the Seasons

The sun's angle changes through the seasons and varies with the time of day. Take this into account as you plan your deck.

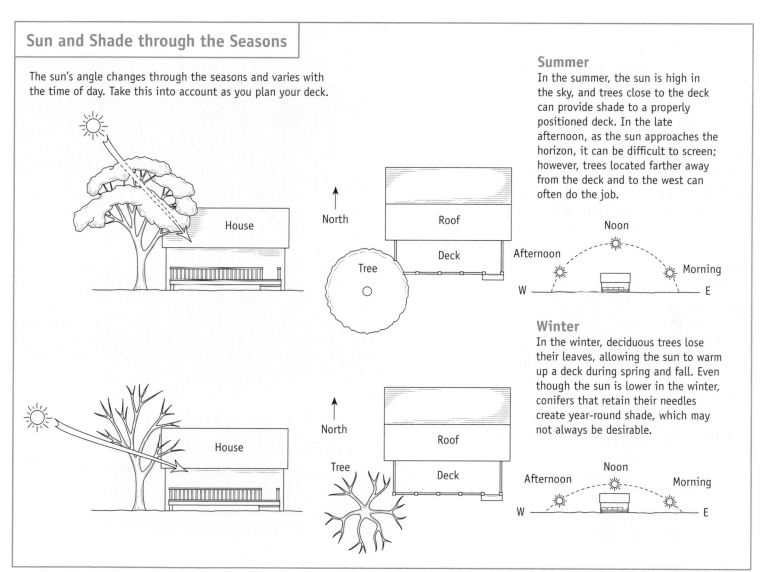

Summer
In the summer, the sun is high in the sky, and trees close to the deck can provide shade to a properly positioned deck. In the late afternoon, as the sun approaches the horizon, it can be difficult to screen; however, trees located farther away from the deck and to the west can often do the job.

Winter
In the winter, deciduous trees lose their leaves, allowing the sun to warm up a deck during spring and fall. Even though the sun is lower in the winter, conifers that retain their needles create year-round shade, which may not always be desirable.

Like the sun, the **wind** can be a welcome visitor or a bothersome intruder. Cooling summer breezes can make an otherwise uncomfortable spot pleasant, while the frequently raw winds of spring and fall can chill you to the bone. You can use solid walls and fences or even portions of the house to shield you from the wind, or choose open-style railings to allow the breezes to flow freely. A word of caution: If you plan to install a privacy screen but don't want to block the summer breezes, choose a style that is visually solid but still allows air through—such as one with spaced vertical boards installed on an angle.

There's something magical about being outside but under cover, watching and listening to the **rain**. If this appeals to you, find a way to include that opportunity. One way is to have a screened porch adjacent to your deck. Other options include building a watertight pergola, adding a deep overhang to your house, or installing a retractable awning.

At nearly 8 ft. tall, these glass panels are an unobtrusive way to block undesirable gusts of wind. Keep in mind that to be kept clean they have to be washed regularly and they might pose a hazard for wildlife and humans alike.

This stylish, retractable canopy uses standard waterproof umbrella fabric. It's supported by a center rail and can be moved manually or with the aid of a remote-controlled, motorized system.

Types of Overhead Structures

Overhead structures and covers not only provide protection from the weather, most notably the sun, but they can also add style to your deck. They can be fixed, movable, or retractable features.

UMBRELLAS
$

- Portable
- Available in various sizes, fabrics, and colors
- Cast a small shadow but can be moved, and some models tilted, to be more effective
- Usually have to be lowered or brought indoors during periods of high winds

PERGOLAS AND ARBORS
$$–$$$

- Permanent fixtures that typically consist of two to four posts that support an open, trellis-like "roof"
- Can be made of wood, composite materials, or metal
- Custom-built or ordered in precut kits
- Can be covered with fabric

AWNINGS
$$–$$$

- Typically attach to the house at the eave or roof
- Fixed or retractable options
- Support poles placed at the outer corners extend the reach of fixed awnings
- Available in a wide range of fabrics and colors

SAILS
$$–$$$

- Create shade for areas of the deck away from the house
- Supported with guy wires
- Available in a range of fabrics and colors

These flanking pergolas have thin, widely spaced purlins, which are set up on edge so that they won't sag over time. Note the minimal amount of shade they create as well as the interesting pattern on the house wall.

Overhead Structures and Coverings

It's probably safe to say that just about everyone enjoys the feeling of the sun shining down and warming us up. But let's face it, too much of a good thing can be, well, too much, and the midsummer sun can drive us into the shade. That's particularly true with today's concerns about sun overexposure. The rain, too, can thwart our outdoor enjoyment. By including an overhead structure or covering as a part of your deck, you won't have to evacuate your deck to avoid the elements.

1. Suspended from guy wires and available in a variety of shapes, sails are an artistic way to add shade to a deck. They are often used over locations that would be difficult to shade by other methods or structures. 2. The translucent quality of fabrics permits light to pass through while mitigating the direct rays of the sun. Heat can still build up under an awning, so be sure to choose light colors to reflect as much sun as possible and perhaps install a fan to disperse the excess heat. 3. Vine-covered pergolas and trellises offer a couple of advantages over their man-made relatives. Their au naturale shade has a built-in cooling effect, and in the fall, when additional sunlight is welcome, they lose their leaves. 4. Retractable awnings are effective at combating the elements in an instant. This model is designed to be installed on overhead tracks. When not in use, it folds discreetly up against the wall. 5. Although their area is generally small, umbrellas are a great way to generate flexible, spot shading. This oversized, cantilever model gets the typical support pole out of the way so that it's easier to position the chaise lounges for optimal protection. 6. In addition to providing shade, pergolas can also be used to identify space. Along with the level changes and railing, the four posts of this pergola separate the dining area from the rest of the deck.

A Deck for Sun, Shade, and Shelter

As frustrating as it is to forecast, there's at least one certainty about the weather—it's changeable. Even if you live in a part of the country where the weather is relatively constant, the outdoor environment changes with the hours of the day. The pleasant morning sun, the boiling rays at noon, or a quick cloudburst may all visit your deck during the course of a single day. With a little foresight, your deck can be fully prepared for whatever nature throws at it.

This deck, located in a sun-blessed part of the country, is a case in point. When the current owners bought the house, the south-facing, sunnyside deck was a plus. However, without any type of overhead protection, it was at the mercy of the elements. To make the deck more livable throughout the seasons, they decided on a three-pronged approach. They left the eastern side uncovered, allowing the morning sun to shine unobstructed on the breakfast table, but covered the middle and western sections to provide varying degrees of protection. To visually tie everything together, the existing deck was stained, and the newly added covers and their supports were styled and detailed to match the house.

Appropriately thick columns support the covered section, and the solid roof shelters those on the deck from the rain as well as the sun. The wooden valance that stretches from column to column conceals retractable shades.

When the ambient temperature is too high for comfort and the mere act of breathing makes you break out in a sweat, this ceiling fan will come to the rescue. On the other hand, when the winds kick up, the shades can be lowered to calm things down.

The pergola's purlins are fairly close together, which means they can create shade but also allow light to filter through.

Designed to blend with the style of home, the deck adds architectural interest and enhances what was once a relatively bland side of the house. Over the years, the small saplings at the east and west corners will grow up to provide additional summertime shade.

Size and Shape

While your budget will certainly have a lot to say about the size and complexity of your deck, there is an old architectural expression—form follows function—that is particularly relevant when it comes to planning and designing decks. In fact, this saying might be amended to say, "*Size and shape* follow function." In other words, as you plan your deck, let the types of activities you'll use it for and their required accessories help guide your decisions (see the sidebar on p. 103). Let's consider size first.

When outside, we typically "live larger" than we do when we are indoors, so using interior spaces to guide the size of your deck can be misleading. Generally, decks require more circulation space around tables and chairs, and some types of furniture, such as chaise lounges, can take up more space than you might think. Decks that are used for entertaining will probably need to accommodate many more people than your living room, so including extra space for those events, even if they are infrequent, shouldn't necessarily be viewed as wasted.

Conventional thinking might have the size of your house dictate the size of your deck, believing that a small deck will look out of place on a large house and a large one will overwhelm a small house. At first blush this might seem true, but careful planning should be able to make almost any size deck look and feel right on any home. For example, to make small decks appear larger and more substantial, employ strategies such as using narrow decking, heavy railings, and wide stairs. You can also extend a small deck's footprint with a wide band of low plantings around its edges. Conversely, a large deck can be brought to the proper scale by using wider decking and visually lighter railings and by breaking it up with multiple levels and/or bump-outs. But be careful not to make the resulting deck sections so small that they fail to function as intended.

Instead of meeting at 90 degrees, this corner was angled to form a bump-out and make enough room for a dining area.

Save a Tree

Instead of cutting down a tree that may be smack-dab in the middle of your deck plans, build around it. Incorporating a tree into your deck can make for a nice design feature, and it can also function as a natural source of shade.

The two curved sections of this multilevel deck are sized and shaped to reflect their uses. The smaller upper section hosts dining-in-the-round off to the side but when necessary can co-opt the other portion of the deck. The curve of the lower deck emulates the fire pit, and although the built-in bench may appear too far away, that's not likely to be the case when the fire is roaring.

Decks, by their nature, are relatively simple structures, which may be why some folks have a strong
temptation to jazz things up by adding lots of
unusual shapes. While there's nothing necessarily
wrong with that, it's a good idea to avoid making
arbitrary choices or including shapes just to be
different. Instead, let the shape of your deck be a
natural reflection of how the space will be used.
For example, bumping out an octagonal shape to
accommodate a round dining table or including a
long, narrow rectangle to provide an out-of-the-way
space for a lounge chair makes perfect sense. Creating angles or turning sections of a deck can also be
an effective way to improve a view or alter the traffic
flow patterns.

Natural features in the surrounding landscape can
also influence the shape of your deck. For example,
you might want to angle your deck so that it offers a
view of an interesting rock formation or even build
the deck so that it actually touches the outcropping.
Mature trees can also shape your deck. To avoid
potential harm or damage, you might decide to
build your deck around them. Another approach is
to incorporate the tree, surrounding it with the deck
(see the sidebar on p. 101).

The plan for your deck may be influenced by
setback restrictions—the closest distance to your
property line that you can build. Familiarize yourself
with the local zoning regulations and homeowner
association restrictions before you get too far in the
planning process.

facing page • Space can be at a premium on rooftop decks, so every little bit extra can make a big difference on the usability scale. Bumping the deck out slightly created just enough room to shift the chairs out of the way of the door.

below • Anything but a simple square or rectangular deck would look odd on this symmetrical, modern-style home.

Providing Adequate Space for Activity Areas

Use the following guidelines to help ensure that your deck has adequate space for its planned uses. Another more hands-on approach is to take a tape measure with you when you visit friends and write down the dimensions of their decks and clearances.

SITTING AND LOUNGING AREAS

Account for the size of the chairs, and provide 2 ft. to 3 ft. of clearance to the front and the sides. One foot to 2 ft. between the chairs should be adequate, unless you need more room for an occasional coffee table.

EATING AREAS

You'll need space for the table plus 3 ft. to 5 ft. on all sides. Large dining-size chairs that might not slide far under the table need more space, while the typically smaller chairs used at bistro tables require less.

COOKING AREAS

The space needs for these areas vary widely depending on the type and amount of equipment. A simple grill only requires space for the unit (grills seem to be getting larger and larger, so plan for those potential upgrades) as well as enough circulation space—4 ft. to 5 ft.—around it for the cook and inevitable "sous chefs." For cooking areas that include other appliances and countertops, follow the guidelines used for indoor kitchens: Counters should be 2 ft. deep; there should be a minimum of 1 ft. of counter space on either side of a sink or cooking surface; and there should be a minimum of 3 ft. between a counter and a wall, 4 ft. between two counters, and 5 ft. between opposite counters in a U-shaped layout.

HOT TUBS AND SPAS

In addition to accounting for the size of the tub or spa, the amount of additional required space depends on where it's located. If it's slipped into an out-of-the-way corner with access limited to one or two sides, provide enough space (2 ft. to 3 ft.) on the closed sides for folks to sit up out of the water. When positioned more out in the open, leave at least a few feet between the tub or spa and the main travel area, and leave enough space around them for lounging.

POOLS

Lounge chairs, of course, line the sides of most pools, so be sure to plan for adequate space, 4 ft. or more, between the pool edge and front of the chairs. Although it's not absolutely necessary, allocating a few feet behind will make the deck feel spacious and allow the furniture to be easily rearranged. Other furniture and equipment, such as tables and grills, are a part of a poolside deck, so be sure to plan accordingly.

Creating an Outdoor Room

If you want to add outdoor living space but would like the deck
to feel more like an extension of your house, rather than wide
open, you can create an outdoor room. One important thing to
consider is its size. To feel like a part of the house, your outdoor
room should be an appropriate scale, as is the case with this one
that's tucked into the corner of a modest home. It's not so large as
to overwhelm the house, nor is it so small that it doesn't function
as intended. Other issues to keep in mind are creating a sense
of enclosure, both on the sides of the deck and overhead, and
choosing a color scheme.

right • Movable shades make it possible to "wall
in" this outdoor room when the sun is low
in the sky, when the breeze may be a bit too
strong, or when more privacy is desired.

right • Although the deck's
"doorway" is larger than an
interior door, its scale is in
keeping with the size of the
space—the yard—it leads to.
A large square mirror adds
a unique unifying touch,
seemingly bringing the
outdoors inside.

above • Placing the furniture off to the sides creates a center "hall" and maximizes the use of space. There's room for a bistro table and chairs, a long couch, and a couple of lounge chairs.

left • The white-painted elements—railings, posts, and pergola—integrate this outdoor room with the home's window trim, shutters, blinds, and even the gutters.

Style and Color

An important part of planning and designing your deck is choosing the style. A good way to begin is to look to your house for cues about elements, such as railing type, trim and stair details, and color scheme. Decks added to homes that have a distinct architectural style of their own—such as an ornate Victorian or a sleek modern house—will perhaps be most successful if they mimic, or blend with, the existing style and level of detail. However, because decks typically host a more informal lifestyle, replicating certain things precisely, such as fancy turned balusters and fluted posts, can make a deck feel overdone. But rules are made to be broken, and you might devise a mixed scheme that works for your house.

Many of the houses built since the 1950s are architecturally stripped down, or incorporate a mix of architectural styles, and have far less and much simpler detailing. When it comes to designing a deck, this can be a blessing in disguise. Such a house can be viewed as a blank canvas ready to accept a wide range of styles. You might take the existing details and pump them up so that your deck enhances your house style. Or you might create a completely different style for your deck. Just make sure the deck doesn't overwhelm the house.

With the proliferation of available hardwood and synthetic decking and the various railing types and systems, color is an element of deck style that has recently gained more attention. As with other details, when deciding on a color scheme, you can choose one that blends with or contrasts with your house. But make sure that your color choice doesn't work against something else you're trying to accomplish. For example, if you want your railing to visually disappear, it's not a good idea to paint the balusters a bright color. Even white, when contrasted against a dark-colored decking, can be distracting.

Wooden decking can be left natural and finished with a clear sealer or stained to a specific color. Either way, it will require regular refinishing. Painting wooden decking is typically not a good idea; it can wear off quickly and is difficult to refinish. Synthetic decking comes in various colors, and its manufacturers tout the colorfastness of their products. Matching railing systems are available for many types of synthetic decking.

above • Minimalism is the password here. The entire railing system—the narrow top rail, cable wire infill, and thin supporting posts—is whittled down, intended to visually step out of the way and let the important thing, the view, take center stage.

above • A zippy shade of blue snaps these railings and balusters to life, setting up a vibrant background for the coordinated, bold red seat cushions and umbrella.

above • Picking up on the color scheme employed on the exterior of the house, the deck's brown posts match the corner boards and window trim, while the light-colored top rail echos that of the siding. The dark metal balusters almost disappear.

left • The house trim, railing system, and even the furniture are cloaked with the same rich green paint, but perhaps what's most striking about this deck are the posts. With their wide profile, paneled sides, and detailed bases and caps, they look more like fine woodwork than railing posts.

Built-Ins

Incorporating built-ins—such as benches, storage containers, and planters—is an effective way to personalize your deck while at the same time making it more functional. Built-ins are space-efficient and can be customized to precisely match the style of your deck. They can be constructed with the same high-quality, rot-resistant materials and fasteners that are used for the rest of the deck.

Built-ins can be used to separate and differentiate various deck spaces, or rooms, but, as the name suggests, built-ins are fixed in their positions on the deck and should be carefully planned. If a built-in will be integrated into the deck structure, its location and configuration will probably need to be determined during the deck's planning phase. Those that sit on top of the decking can be placed after the decking is installed and their exact position fine-tuned by using mockups.

above • Ingeniously disguised as a built-in planter, the open door gives up its true identity—a waterproof storage locker. The planters fronting the secret cubbyhole do their part by hiding it and lessening its visual impact.

below • The built-in benches on this small deck do double duty as end tables when they're not in use as additional seating during social gatherings.

Although curves are time-consuming and expensive to execute, the extra effort and additional cost are usually rewarded with stunning results, as demonstrated by the curved wooden bench and railing that grace this deck.

BENCHES

Benches are perhaps the most common type of deck built-in and come in a wide array of styles. They can be short and straight, long and curved, form 90-degree inside corners, or wrap around an outside corner. They can have backs or not, and the seats and backs can be straight or angled. Benches are often located at the deck perimeter, where they double as low railings, and are a great way to provide seating for a large number of people within a relatively small footprint. However, benches may face away from a nice view, so keep that in mind when planning your bench location. Consider other places that might benefit from a solid, built-in bench, such as near a door for sitting on to remove shoes or around a hot tub to create an area where people can talk or even stretch out and take a nap.

Although benches appear inviting and romantic, they all too often become uncomfortable after sitting on them for a few minutes. Building a comfortable bench you'll want to linger on requires thoughtful design. To begin, think about how the bench will be used and by whom. Backless benches provide little or no lumbar support and may be tiring to sit on for long periods of time. While bench backs can increase the level of comfort, unless the relationship between the seat and the back is appropriate, they can still be uncomfortable. And if a bench will be used in conjunction with a table, the relationship between the two is also important. To make sure your bench is one you will enjoy sitting on, it's not a bad idea to find one you like and have it duplicated.

Built-in benches can be designed with flip-up seats and used for storage. An extremely long bench can be a bit aesthetically boring, with the same profile stretching on for feet upon feet. Interspersing such a bench with planters or small occasional tables can break up the monotony. Benches can also be built in conjunction with arbors or pergolas.

Without any visible means of support, this thick plank bench apparently "grows" out from the built-in planter, which forms a low back. The bench extends beyond the planter, is cut to the correct thickness, and becomes one of the stair treads.

Bench Backs

On decks that are 30 in. or more above ground, building codes require some type of guard, typically a 36-in.-high railing, at the edges of the deck. To meet this requirement when using a built-in bench at an edge of your deck, the back should be 36 in. high or, if it's backless, have a railing behind it. Some inspectors might interpret it differently and measure 36 in. from the seat, so be sure to check with your local officials. Even if your jurisdiction doesn't have this requirement, following this guideline will increase your deck's safety.

above · This backless bench provides ample, if simple, seating and guards the edge of the on-grade but somewhat elevated deck. Its unassuming profile, evident when viewed from the ground, is similar to but narrower than the deck's.

below · Instead of interrupting the long lines of this bench with planters or tables to alleviate its uniformity, the privacy screen, which springs up from the lower railing, does the trick.

Built-In Benches

Often integrated with the structure, built-in benches are functional and add a visual, almost sculptural element to decks. Their style is as varied as the decks they inhabit. They can be simple, backless planks or highly designed with sloping seats and backs. Typically made of wood or synthetic planks, their hard seats can be made more comfortable with the addition of cushions. When used in conjunction with a table, the seat height and depth dimensions should be carefully calculated to ensure a comfortable relationship.

1. A much less costly way to capture the feeling that a curved bench creates is to build one that's multisided. You can shape the space benches define by adjusting the lengths of each side and altering the angle at which they meet. 2. Right-angle corners can be uncomfortable, if not impossible, places to sit. Replacing the seat with a table or planter turns what would be wasted space into an asset. 3. When closed at the bottom and constructed with solid backs, benches can also be used as privacy screens. Outfitting such a bench with a hinged top gives it yet another use as a storage unit. 4. To minimize the number of structural members, these beefy supports—the angled back and horizontal seat pieces—are integrated with the railing posts. 5. Painted to match the trim, this built-in bench makes the most of space and an unusual opportunity. The seat back, which is shingled to drive home the point, is actually part of a wall of the screened porch. 6. Located next to the hot tub, this right-angle bench is positioned perfectly for toweling off or taking a cool-down break. Shifting one leg to the bench and having it replace a section of railing uncovered additional floor space.

PLANTERS

Built-in planters are great if you want to add an unusually shaped or particularly long planter to your deck. They can stand alone or be incorporated with built-in benches.

Built-in planters are an effective way to delineate a stairway or other transitional areas. When filled with plants that have thick foliage, they make excellent privacy screens. Planting evergreens, or combining a planter with a trellis or arbor, can provide year-round privacy. One unique way to use a built-in planter as a privacy screen is as the back of a bench. This can work particularly well on a multilevel deck that has a bench or seating area located at an area where the level changes. The planter acts as a wall, shielding the view of the seating area from the level above.

When planning for built-in planters, you should think about the types of plants you want to use, how they grow, and what size they'll be so the planters can accommodate the spatial needs of the plants (see pp. 188–190).

above right · A mix of square and rectangular planters brings a country feel to this rooftop city deck. The two shrubs would benefit from some regular pruning to keep them in scale with their planters and surroundings.

right · Filling this diamond-shaped built-in planter, even partway, would require a lot of soil. Using potted plants instead can yield the same results with a lot less hauling and mess.

This planter's graceful curve not only escorts people along the edge of the deck but also acts as a low guard. Although the distance to the lower deck might require a code-height railing, the planting bed is above that deck, thereby negating that requirement and allowing the upper deck to feel more spacious.

STORAGE

To help overcome the ongoing storage challenge most of us face, take an inventory of everything you will use on your deck and determine what kind of outdoor storage is needed. Grill-dedicated cooking utensils and equipment, all-weather place mats and tablecloths, trivets, and tableware are prime candidates. Cushions, if they will accompany your chairs or benches, can present a dilemma. Even if they are weatherproof, they can retain moisture, so you will probably want to protect them from the rain and even the morning dew. Otherwise, you'll have to let them dry before sitting on them. Nearby, on-deck storage makes stowing these bulky items a breeze. Storing children's toys or even sports equipment on your deck can eliminate multiple trips to the playroom or garage to retrieve just the right thing.

Once you've identified what you want to store, determine which configuration—horizontal or vertical storage—would be best the best option. Horizontal storage boxes, bins, and benches are great for holding bulky items such cushions, balls, and bags of charcoal. However, smaller items can get lost in the jumble. Putting those things in smaller containers can help, but a better solution might be a storage cabinet with adjustable shelves. No matter what type of unit you choose, make sure that it's large enough so that you don't have to stuff or squeeze things into place.

Deck storage can either be built-in or portable. The most common type of built-in storage is bench storage, but there's no reason you couldn't have custom-made fixed bins or cabinets. However, because your storage needs may change over time, it might make sense to buy manufactured, portable storage units. They come in many different styles, materials (wood, synthetics, and even all-weather wicker), and sizes. Some are designed specifically for storing cushions, and others have wheels and handles so they can easily be moved out of the way during large gatherings. Other types can be folded up for off-season storage; if you're handy, you can purchase a put-together kit.

Whether you go the built-in or manufactured route, with natural or synthetic materials, your storage containers should be waterproof—even if what you're storing won't be affected if it gets wet—and ventilated so that the water doesn't get trapped inside and inevitably condense and cause mold or mildew.

To store really large items, such as furniture or even garden equipment, take a look under your deck. If you have enough headroom and you will not be using that space as living space, consider creating some under-deck storage. There are two approaches you can take—putting individual storage containers under the deck or turning a large portion or the entire area into a storage unit.

With either option, it's a good idea to make the under-deck area a more inviting place. Level it as much as possible, and consider covering the dirt with $\frac{3}{8}$-in. to $\frac{1}{2}$-in. washed stone or perhaps concrete paving stones. If the ground is very moist, consider installing a waterproof membrane, such as 6-mil black plastic, under the stones.

To ensure a watertight area, install metal roofing below a standard deck. To hide the stored items from view, consider skirting (see pp. 48–49) around the perimeter of the deck. If you go this route, be sure to provide for ventilation because moisture can build up.

left and below • Say the magic words—abracadabra, presto-change-o, open sesame—and this non-assuming deck skirt parts to reveal a hidden feature—a cleverly designed storage facility. Although not tall, it's the perfect shape and size to accommodate these kayaks.

below • Look closely and you'll notice that a section of the skirting is actually a hinged door. The closely spaced latticework and under-deck darkness keep what's stored there, no matter how messy it might be, discreetly out of sight.

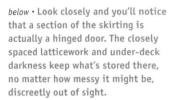

DETAILS THAT WORK

Seats That Store

Storage units don't have to be elaborate to be effective. Tossing small items into this bin, perhaps children's toys, can be made into a game of basketball and when the game is over and the cover in place, it makes a great seat for at least one of the participants.

Planning Your Deck   **117**

Lighting

One important aspect of deck planning and design that all too often gets treated as an afterthought is lighting. If you intend to use your deck in the hours after the sun goes down, or even just walk across it in the dark to get somewhere, adequate and effective lighting is essential. In addition to making your deck safer and more enjoyable, exterior deck lighting will improve the view from inside your house, eliminating the "black mirror" that's created when there is no exterior illumination, and allowing you to enjoy your deck and landscape.

There are three basic types of lighting to choose from—solar, low voltage, and high voltage. **Solar** lighting, as the name suggests, gets its power from the sun. It is easy to install, typically can be placed and moved anywhere, and it turns itself on without the need for a switch. Although not as bright as low- or high-voltage lighting, solar lighting can be effectively used as part of an overall lighting scheme.

Low-voltage lights are powered by a voltage transformer (reducer) that is typically plugged into a house receptacle. Individual low-voltage fixtures, which are smaller and less obtrusive than their high-voltage counterparts, are connected in a series with wires. Fixtures can be purchased separately or as part of a kit. Low-voltage lighting can be installed by do-it-yourselfers, and it's relatively easy to change the fixture locations. Low-voltage lighting doesn't provide as much light as a high-voltage system.

High-voltage lighting uses standard household current and usually requires a dedicated circuit. High-voltage lighting is more costly to install and should be installed by a licensed professional. It provides the strongest light possible, and there is a wide range of available fixtures.

A good, balanced lighting scheme will usually incorporate more than one type of lighting, lighting fixtures, and lighting techniques (see the sidebar on p. 120) for an effect called "light layering." Building codes typically require the illumination of stairs—both the steps and landings. Because local codes differ, it's a good idea to verify with the building or wiring inspector the exact requirements you'll have to meet.

above • Unobtrusive but effective, the small post fixtures cast their light downward, softly illuminating the deck's perimeter. Given how wide the steps are, they would probably be safer if riser lights had been installed in a few more locations.

above • A mix of lighting that includes post lamps, railing down lights, and landscape lighting combine to make this deck an inviting place to approach at night.

Types of Light Bulbs

There are several types of light bulbs, called lamps in the industry, available to light your deck. Each has its pluses and minuses, which you should evaluate carefully when making your choices.

STANDARD INCANDESCENTS
$

- Relatively short life—about 750 hours
- Inexpensive and readily available
- Produced in a wide range of wattages
- Easily dimmed
- Light yellows when dimmed
- Least energy-efficient lamp available

HALOGENS (OR QUARTZ LAMPS)
$$

- Long life—about 2,500 to 3,000 hours
- More energy efficient than standard incandescents
- Smaller fixtures
- Light can be focused to a narrow beam
- Light yellows and life can be shortened when dimmed
- Can get very hot—fires have been attributed to some types
- Hot bulbs should not be touched without gloves on

COMPACT FLUORESCENTS
$$

- Long life—about 10,000 to 20,000 hours
- Very energy efficient—give three to five times the light output per watt compared with standard incandescents

- Produce less heat
- Don't change color when dimmed
- Improved color rendition and reduced size
- Newer types have built-in ballasts
- Light output diminishes with age
- Larger than standard incandescents and may not fit in all fixtures
- Light quality is usually slightly different than incandescent light
- Ballasts in inexpensive lamps may hum or buzz

LOW VOLTAGE
$$-$$$

- Long life—about 10,000 hours
- Uses 12-volt current and reduces potential for shocks
- Produces about two and a half times more light than a 110-volt fixture
- Fixtures are expensive—about two to four times more than conventional fixtures
- Most need a separate transformer to reduce the 110-volt line current down to 12 volts

LIGHT-EMITTING DIODES (LED)
$$$

- Extremely long life—about 100,000 hours
- Extremely energy efficient—uses less energy than other types of bulbs
- Does not produce as much light as incandescent or compact fluorescent bulbs
- Uses standard 110-volt current

The uplights shining on the trees surrounding this deck not only high-light the trees but also create a sense of safety by extending the visual field beyond the edges of the deck.

Post-Cap Lights

Post-cap lights are just that—post caps with lights built into them. These two-for-one items give life to otherwise bare posts and shed light to your deck. Designed to fit on the top of a 4x4 post, the wiring for this light is fed from underneath the deck up through the post.

Lighting Techniques and Effects

Effective lighting isn't just about the type of lighting and mix of fixtures. There are several lighting techniques and effects you can choose from to create a beautiful and safe nighttime deck environment.

- **Ambient lighting:** This is a general type of light that is created indoors by bouncing light off of walls and ceilings. This effect is harder to achieve outdoors, but light can be reflected off of house walls and overhead structures, such as pergolas and awnings.

- **Shadowing:** Use this technique to highlight interesting shapes, like a large plant or the branch structure of a tree. Place the light source in front of the object, and aim it so that a shadow is cast on a surface such as a wall or board fence.

- **Silhouetting:** Use this technique to outline and emphasize the shape of an object like a tree or an overhead structure. Place the light source behind the object, and shine the light against a solid surface like a wall or fence.

- **Moonlighting:** To achieve this ambient lighting effect, place the light source up in a tree and shine the light down through the branches. The resulting shadows will make it appear that the moon is shining.

- **Vignetting:** Train several light sources toward a single spot to highlight a specific location or object.

- **Task lighting:** This type of focused, bright lighting is a necessity in outdoor kitchens. When placing task lighting overhead, be sure not to position it behind where the cook will be standing or it will cast shadows on the work surface.

- **Safety lighting:** In addition to any code-required safety lighting, you may want to provide light where there's a level change or solid, built-in objects. Choose fixtures that cast their light downward or across the surface so that it doesn't shine in one's eyes.

Wall-mounted lanterns light up the doorways that lead out to the deck and throw enough light to enjoy dinner under the stars. The flickering light of the fire is all that's needed to illuminate the area around the fire pit.

Lighting

Attached to walls, hung from pergolas, supported on pillars, and built into steps and posts—there's virtually a light designed for every conceivable situation. To beautifully and safely light your deck and the surrounding landscape, you will no doubt need to select more than one type. Most of us are not as familiar with exterior lighting as we are with interior lighting, so it might be helpful to actually see some examples of outdoor lighting in action.

1. Low-voltage fixtures can be small, which is a big plus when it comes to decks because many of their components are small too. The thin wire that powers this fixture is hidden in holes drilled up from the bottom and in from the side of this stair railing post. 2. Wall-hung fixtures may produce sufficient light to adequately illuminate relatively small decks. Fixtures that allow light to shine out to the sides, without excessive glare, will do a better job than those that only direct their light downward. 3. A stately pair of gas lamps, built into the tops of the dry-stacked, concrete block pillars, signals the entrance to this fireplace deck. Similar lamps perched on the shoulders of the fireplace add their light to that of the fire. 4. Talk about being creative—the patterns of light shining through these risers give a whole new meaning to the word. Although the designs may appear to be random, the arrangement is tied together by every other riser, which have the same light pattern.

5. Stairs are hazardous enough in the daytime, and nighttime exacerbates the problem. Providing ample and effective lighting is crucial to help avoid missteps and falls. 6. Overhead structures offer the opportunity to conceal wires and hang heavy fixtures. However, this lightweight paper globe can easily be unplugged and moved indoors during the off-season or even if particularly violent weather is in the forecast. 7. Lighting affords you the opportunity to be inventive. These posts, which mark the entrance to the steps and entry deck beyond, are hollow and the fronts have been cut away and faced with translucent lenses, which let the light shine out. The top rails are inset with light-emitting acrylic rods.

ELEMENTS

With a few exceptions, all decks share the same basic elements—framing components,

decking, railings, and stairs. Having a general understanding of these items will

help you communicate with your builder when the talk turns technical.

OF A DECK

Framing Components

While most of us look closely at the finish work of decking and railings, a deck's framing members are just as important. In fact, because they are exposed to the elements, and often in plain sight, structural components need special attention. Although rare, deck failures and accidents due to structural deficiencies do happen. So if you need to trim costs, you should look someplace other than on structure.

Intricate decking patterns and heavy items such as hot tubs may require additional framing and blocking; be sure to plan ahead.

PIERS AND POSTS

Piers provide a stable surface on which to build a structure and support the weight of that structure. Deck piers are typically concrete poured into 8-in.- to 12-in.-dia. cylindrical forms, but can also be made from concrete blocks. The number of piers and the distance between them is determined by the way the deck is framed, the design load (total weight) of the deck, and your soil's bearing capacity (the load that soil can support without failing). To distribute the weight they carry, piers should be installed on footings. In areas of the country that freeze, footings must be installed below the frost line.

Posts are vertical members, usually made of pressure-treated or rot-resistant wood, that rest on the piers and support the deck's floor structure—beams and joists. Steel posts, or lally columns, are sometimes used in modern designs. Wood is relatively strong along its length, so 4x4 posts are often strong enough to do the job. However, 4x4s can be visually weak and appear spindly, so from a design perspective, using 6x6 or even 8x8 posts often makes sense. To dress them up, rough posts can be covered with finish boards.

top right • In a break from typical deck construction, the ends of these floor joists are left exposed and project beyond the plane of the decking. At 3 in. thick, twice the thickness of a standard joist, they have the visual weight to make a bold statement.

facing page • Exposed metal is the theme for this railing system, which includes a galvanized pipe handrail and coated wire infill. The posts are secured with heavy-duty, custom-made galvanized steel brackets.

right • The concrete piers that support this deck extend above the ground, eliminating the need for posts. The beam is secured to the piers with metal brackets imbedded in the concrete.

Framing Hardware

Another structural necessity that you should pay attention to is the hardware—bolts, hangers, brackets, and screws—that are needed to hold your deck together. With typical deck construction, many of these are visible. So be sure you know what parts you will or will not see and, if something is going to bother your aesthetics, talk to your builder about a way to hide it or at least minimize its effect.

BEAMS, LEDGERS, AND FLOOR JOISTS

Beams and ledgers support the deck's floor joists. They, too, are made of pressure-treated wood and sit horizontally on top of, or are notched into, the posts and secured with special hardware or bolts. When on-grade decks are close enough to the ground, 8 in. to 12 in., the beams are laid directly on top of the concrete piers, eliminating the need for posts.

Ledgers are attached to the foundation or frame of the house. This structural member can fail if not constructed properly. It must be secured to the house with enough properly sized lag screws or bolts to prevent it from pulling away from the house. Additionally, flashing, a thin waterproof material, must be properly applied at the joint between the ledger and the house so that water cannot infiltrate that space and cause rot and corrosion.

Floor joists form the floor structure of the deck and support for the decking material. Individual joists, depending on how far they span, are 2x8s, 2x10s, or 2x12s. They are usually installed perpendicular to the house and, depending on the thickness and type of decking, either 16 in. or 24 in. apart. If the floor joists run over the tops of the beams, not into their faces or sides, the ends of the floor joists are tied together with band joists, a joist-size board that runs perpendicular to the joists. Depending on the type of system, railing posts may be fastened to the beams or the band joists.

above right • Two decks are better than one. Instead of building one tall, elevated deck the homeowners decided to maximize space by building a small, intimate upper deck and a larger lower deck to accommodate gatherings.

right • Structural components don't need to look the part. These posts, rails, and braces all add to the beauty of the deck and the home.

Typical Deck Framing

Although the precise type, number, and location of structural components vary from deck to deck, the basics are typically the same.

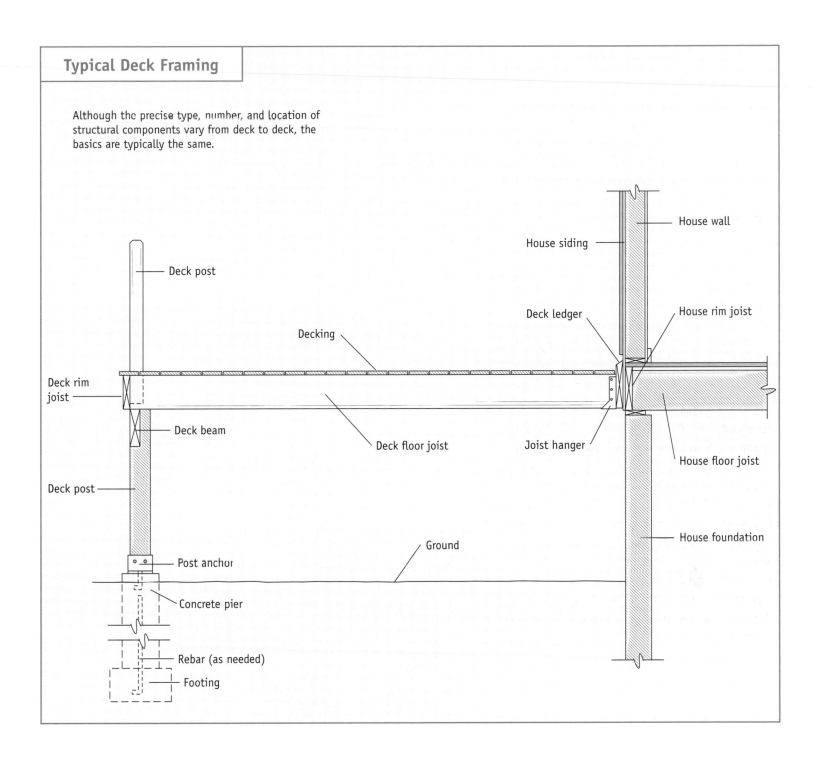

House wall

House siding

Deck post

Decking

Deck ledger

House rim joist

Deck rim joist

Deck beam

Deck floor joist

Joist hanger

House floor joist

Deck post

House foundation

Ground

Post anchor

Concrete pier

Rebar (as needed)

Footing

Framed for Function and Beauty

Often during the course of designing an addition or interior renovation, it becomes clear that another part of the house will also have to undergo a transformation to mesh with the new or remodeled space. In this instance, it was the existing deck. As a part of a major kitchen remodel, a long bank of windows and a new door were added to the rear of this house. Plans called for the new kitchen door to lead to the deck, so although the owners knew that the small existing elevated deck would have to be resurfaced and enlarged, the plan was to keep and utilize at least some of the framing.

The homeowners also wanted to include a set of steps that would connect them to the backyard and the basement-level patio underneath the deck. An existing second-floor deck was also flagged for an upgrade. However, when the work began, it was discovered that all of the structural members of both existing decks were too badly rotted to keep. The decks had to be stripped away, and completely new decks were built in their place. Now the homeowners have brand-new, beautifully framed—and, most important, safe—decks.

above • The owners considered building a set of steps to connect the bedroom balcony with the main deck but thought better of it. They wanted to maintain the balcony's "isolation" and also felt that more steps would make things feel cluttered.

right • Halfway down at a landing, the stairs turn at a 45-degree angle. This not only breaks up the long run of stairs, making them safer, but also shifts the steps away from the mature shade tree and closer to the patio.

above • The orderly and crisp lines formed by the deck's posts and railing help to tie the rear elevation together. The newly poured concrete patio extends off to the right and out into the yard a bit, allowing the steps to be located off to the side and out of the way.

above • The spacious main deck has plenty of room for eating and lounging. The furniture blends with the color scheme and the clean lines of the deck's structure.

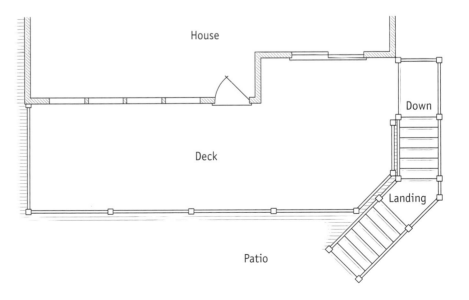

Decking

Perhaps the one part of the deck that has the most visual impact when you're standing on it is the decking itself. The type, color, and installation pattern of material you choose will heavily influence your deck's style, feel, and overall look, so it's important to take your time and weigh all the options carefully.

The plain vanilla approach to installing decking is either parallel with or perpendicular to the house. However, you can choose from a number of other interesting variations and styles. While intricate patterns can spice up your deck, be careful; sometimes you can have too much of a good thing, and a once-attractive pattern can get very busy.

One way to dress up a simple decking installation is to install a border around the outside edge of the deck. Unless your deck is very small, double or triple up the border to make a strong statement.

Decking boards, be they natural wood, composites, or plastic, are typically available in nominal widths of 4 in. and 6 in., which are actually about 3½ in. and 5½ in., respectively. While the wider boards are more commonly used, smaller decks may benefit from the narrower profile of the 4-in. boards—they're more in scale with the deck and make it appear larger.

DETAILS THAT WORK

Decking Borders

The dynamic pattern created by the diagonal decking is, at the same time, tied together and accentuated by the crossed boards installed at intersections. These boards also mask the discrepancies that would be apparent if the decking boards butted into each other.

facing page · Varying the installation direction and intersecting the decking with a pair of curved and contrasting colored boards help to define the spaces on this deck.

right · Introducing color changes is another way to spice up your decking. Here, the curved sections of decking are accentuated by interspersing white boards with brown.

Decking Patterns

As you plan your deck, one major decision you will make is on a decking pattern, and there are many variations to choose from. It can be difficult to visualize the final result, particularly if you're considering using an elaborate pattern or combining two or more patterns, so it can be helpful to look at actual decking installations. Remember that complex decking patterns require extra framing, so make the decision before construction begins.

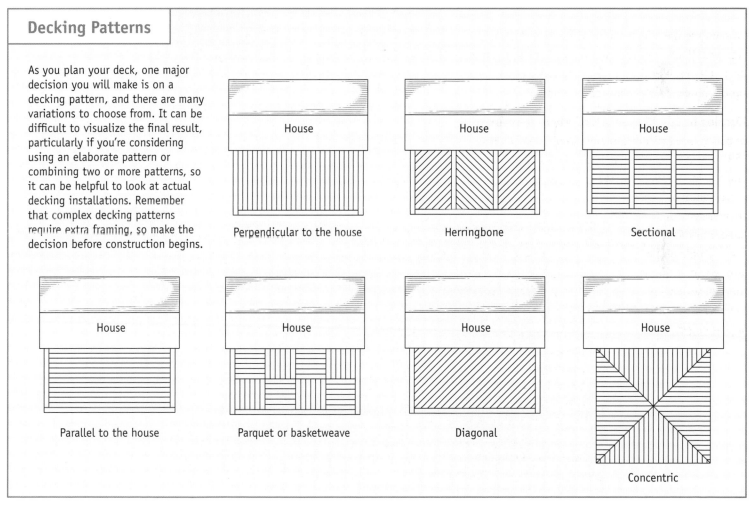

Perpendicular to the house

Herringbone

Sectional

Parallel to the house

Parquet or basketweave

Diagonal

Concentric

A Subtle Definition of Space

There are a number of ways to separate the spaces and uses on a deck—low dividers, screens, and level changes are a few. However, if you'd like some division of space without creating barriers or impediments, a straightforward yet effective strategy is to employ the decking. Simply altering the direction of the decking or introducing a distinctive decking pattern sends the message that each variation indicates a different place on the deck. It's a bit like using area rugs to define spaces in a large room.

The judicious use of decking changes breaks up a large deck and also adds visual interest, but, of course, you don't want to go overboard and create a head-spinning, crazy-quilt effect. You can also include other indicators to accentuate the sense of separation, in this case, the sails overhead and the planter.

right · **The four distinct areas—kitchen/dining, sitting, hot tub, and fire pit—are separated from each other by a change in decking direction, which is laid either parallel or perpendicular to the house. The sails also help to define the spaces.**

The kitchen/dining and sitting areas are located close to the house where they can take advantage of the shade provided by the sails. The hot tub and fire pit seating areas of the deck are located farthest from the house. The hot tub users appreciate the sun, while the fire pit is used at night when the sun is not an issue.

Centered on one of the posts that carries the sails, the built-in planter helps to demarcate the spaces and also signals the way to the steps.

Blessed with a striking view of the Rocky Mountains to the south, the owner of this deck did not want anything to block the scene, so she chose a wide-open, unobstructed plan and decided to let the decking delineate the different areas of the deck. The only tall element—the kitchen counter and pergola—are located off to the side and out of the way.

WOOD DECKING

Historically, when the word "decking" was mentioned, it was wood decking that came to mind. The first decks were constructed with native, rot-resistant woods such as redwood and cedar. These old-growth woods were beautiful but expensive, and as the popularity of decks grew, a less expensive wood—pressure-treated yellow pine—became widely available and quickly dominated the market.

Soon, however, it became apparent that neither of these options was the perfect product. Environmental concerns about turning centuries-old trees into lumber and safety issues with the chemicals used in the pressure-treating process (chromated copper arsenate has been banned for residential use) spurred a search for different decking materials.

As a response, a number of tropical hardwoods slowly became available. These beautiful woods are very rot- and insect-resistant and extremely hard and durable. In addition, changes in the chemicals used in pressure-treated woods and new processes to make wood suitable for outdoor use have added several other wood decking options. One new process, called acetylation, alters the cell structure of the wood to make it resistant to rot, insects, and mold. Thermal modification is another wood-altering process that bakes wood, effectively cooking the sugars within it, making it water insoluble and indigestible to microbes and insects.

The beautiful appearance of wood comes with a hidden cost—maintenance. To keep a wood deck looking new, it must be cleaned and sealed regularly, and brightened (either chemically or with a pressure washer) from time to time. Alternately, you can allow the deck to weather (most woods turn grey) and then regularly apply a preservative.

DETAILS THAT WORK

A Stenciled Design on Wood Decking

Stenciling with paint or stain is an inexpensive way to create the look of an area rug and define a separate space on a wooden deck. Keep in mind that scuffing feet, sliding chairs, and harsh weather will take their toll, so regular touch-ups may be required to keep the design from deteriorating.

below · Ipé, one of numerous tropical hardwoods, is stunning. However, maintaining its dark, rich color requires regular care. The slotted treads make the steps of this deck safer by allowing water to drain through and helping to differentiate the steps from the decks.

Eco-Friendly Wood Decking

The resurgent popularity of decks and the continued desire for wood decking has heightened concerns about overcutting and deforestation. As a result, organizations like the Forest Stewardship Council (FSC) and its Smartwood Program track the harvesting and marketing of trees and lumber, certifying sustainable logging and forest-management practices. When shopping for decking, you can ask if a particular product is FSC certified.

Types of Wood Decking

Not too many years ago, wood decking choices were relatively limited—pressure treated, cedar, and redwood predominated—so making a choice was fairly easy. Now, however, numerous tropical hardwoods and other woods are available, complicating matters. Not all types are available in all areas, so check your local distributors.

RED CEDAR

PRESSURE TREATED
$

- Yellow pine, Hem-fir, Douglas fir
- Inexpensive, strong, and long lasting
- Some varieties can splinter and check
- Low-toxicity preservative available
- Preservative very corrosive to metal fasteners
- Yellow pine readily available in eastern states; Hem-fir and Douglas fir in western states

NATURALLY WEATHER-RESISTANT NATIVE
$–$$

- Redwood, white cedar, red cedar
- Real-wood look
- Soft, subject to dents and scrapes
- Second-growth wood and sapwood not extremely rot- and insect-resistant
- Requires regular cleaning and sealing to maintain color

ACETYLATED
$$–$$$

- Accoya (radiata pine)
- Rot- and insect-resistant
- Stable, paintable
- Sustainable
- Limited availability

THERMALLY MODIFIED
$$–$$$

- Various woods, including southern yellow pine, Douglas fir, red pine, and poplar
- Rot- and insect-resistant
- Stable
- Sustainable
- Limited availability

TROPICAL HARDWOODS
$$$

- Ipé, tigerwood, cumara, garapa, cambara
- Real-wood look—some have stunning grain patterns
- Very strong, rot- and insect-resistant
- Tight grain resists water penetration
- Concerns about deforestation—look for FSC certification

BAMBOO
$$$

- Rapidly renewable resource
- Factory-applied finish cannot be sanded
- Limited availability

COPPER AZOLE

IPÉ

ACCOYA

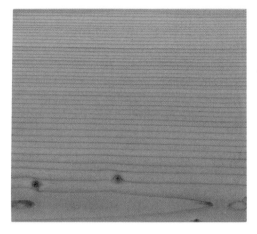

THERMOFOREST

WOLMANIZED

BAMBOO

SYNTHETIC DECKING

There are two general types of synthetic decking—wood and plastic composite (WPC) and solid plastic. Every manufacturer uses a proprietary mix of materials and processes to create its products.

WPC is made from a combination of wood-waste fibers or wood flour and various types of plastics, some of which may be recycled. Solid-plastic decking is made from virgin plastics or a mix of virgin and recycled plastics. While synthetic decking has a number of advantages over wood—it won't rot, splinter, or check and is insect-resistant—the first materials that came out in the early 1990s had issues, including staining, mildew, and, in the case of some WPCs, actual material failure. Although the issues aren't completely resolved, today's products are much improved.

Because it's an alternative to wood decking, synthetic materials mimic the look of wood decking. Not surprisingly, due to their wood component, WPCs do a better job of this than solid-plastic decking, which can be shiny. The wood component also makes WPC stronger than solid-plastic decking; however, under the right conditions, the wood can support mold growth. WPC may also fade. To combat these issues, some manufacturers now cover their products with a protective layer of plastic.

Solid-plastic decking expands and contracts along its length more than wood or WPC decking. Manufacturers typically recommend specific installation methods and details to account for this movement, and some add nonorganic fillers to control expansion. Plastic decking can also get hotter than other materials when exposed to direct sunlight.

Synthetic decking is low maintenance, not maintenance free. While it doesn't need the application of preservatives, synthetic decking does require regular cleaning and some can be sealed.

above · Synthetic decking, railings, and trim boards can be bent, making it easy to create curves.

Synthetics and the Environment

As with wood decking, there are some environmental concerns with synthetic decking. Although wood can theoretically be sustainably harvested, the plastics used in synthetic decking are currently made with a limited resource, oil. Manufacturers who use post-consumer recycled materials consider their products to be "green," but the same cannot be said of the use of virgin plastics. Also, even though synthetic decking is a long-lasting material, nothing lasts forever. At the end of its serviceable life, synthetic decking may find its way to the landfill rather than the compost pile, although some WPC companies are stamping the underside of their boards so they can be returned and recycled. Solid-plastic decking can also potentially be recycled for reuse.

Synthetic decking manufacturers offer a range of colors, posts, and railing systems so it's easy to create a coordinated look.

Types of Synthetic Decking

The world of synthetic decking continues to evolve, and new products are regularly introduced to the marketplace. The same manufacturers often offer more than one type of product, so be sure you understand what you are buying before you buy it.

WOOD-PLASTIC COMPOSITES (WPC)
$–$$
- Weather-, insect-, and splinter-resistant
- Durable but may scratch
- Many contain recycled material
- Low maintenance
- Wood-grain pattern mimics wood
- May fade

POLYVINYL CHLORIDE (PVC)
$$–$$$
- Weather-, insect-, and splinter-resistant
- Lighter than but not as strong as wood or composites
- Fade-resistant
- Low maintenance

COATED (OR CAPPED) WPC AND PVC
$$–$$$
- Combines best features of WPC and PVC
- Wood-grain pattern mimics wood
- Low maintenance
- Expensive

WPC

PVC

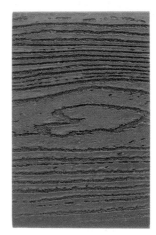

COATED WPC

left · Some of synthetic decking's greatest traits are that it won't rot, splinter, or be penetrated by bugs.

below · Synthetic decking has undergone some major transformations and improvements over the years, and many manufacturers have been able to develop products that imitate wood. This decking was installed with concealed fasteners to maintain an unblemished surface.

ALTERNATIVE DECKING

Although wood and synthetic decking are by far the most common types of deck-surfacing materials, there are several others—such as aluminum, vinyl, fiberglass, outdoor carpeting, and stone or concrete pavers—that you might want to consider. This is particularly true if you are planning an elevated deck that will have outdoor living space underneath it because these decking systems create a waterproof floor system.

Aluminum decking, which is installed directly on top of the floor joists, has an interlocking, gapless profile. Most of the water collects on top of the decking and is directed toward the edge of the deck where it either drops off the edge or into a gutter. The small amount of water that leaks through the decking joints is caught by an integral gutter and also directed away. **Vinyl, fiberglass,** and **outdoor carpeting** are installed on a solid subfloor that is attached to the floor joists. This subfloor is usually made from ¾-in. plywood or other sheet good. One major installation difference between them is that vinyl and fiberglass create a waterproof barrier, while outdoor carpeting must be installed over a waterproof subfloor. As with aluminum decking, water is directed to the edge of the deck. **Stone** and **concrete pavers** are installed in a mortar bed over a waterproof substrate.

For these solid-decking systems to shed water properly, they must pitch away from the house, typically from ⅛ in. to ¼ in. per foot. This can be done in one of two ways—the joists can slope to create the pitch, or, if you want a level ceiling underneath the deck, the top of each joist is cut along its length to create a taper.

above • Natural stone is hard, durable, and long lasting, not to mention beautiful. This light grey sandstone is complemented by the grey railing and stainless steel grill and provides a low-key background upon which to display the wooden table and chairs.

above • Although mainly associated with commercial applications, aluminum decking has found its way into the residential market. Unlike other waterproofing techniques, aluminum decking doesn't require a waterproof substrate and can be installed directly on the floor joists.

Bring a little green to your deck with AstroTURF® type outdoor carpeting. On the plus side, it's inexpensive and durable; however, water doesn't drain or evaporate readily, so it may be wet underfoot for some time after it rains.

Types of Decking Alternatives

Before choosing an alternative type of decking material, weigh the pros and cons carefully. If you are unfamiliar with them, take a field trip and look at some installed examples before making a final decision.

OUTDOOR CARPET
$

- Easy to install
- Low maintenance, easy to clean
- Limited number of colors
- Soft underfoot

VINYL DECKING
$$

- Easy to install
- Low maintenance, easy to clean
- Limited number of colors
- Can be used over finished interior rooms
- High fire rating
- Relatively narrow widths

FIBERGLASS
$$

- Custom/on-site installation
- Easy to clean
- Topcoat may need to be refinished
- Limited number of colors
- Can be used over finished interior rooms

STONE AND CONCRETE PAVERS
$$–$$$

- A wide range of materials and styles
- Certain finishes can be slippery when wet
- Very heavy, may need additional structural support
- Installed in a mortar bed over smooth, waterproof substrate

ALUMINUM DECKING
$$$

- Creates a waterproof deck
- Stronger and lighter than wood, composite, and plastic decking
- Available in long lengths
- Limited number of colors
- Stays cool underfoot

Decking Fasteners

The decking on most early decks was simply secured to the joists with nails driven through the face of boards. However, the constant swelling and shrinking caused by the cycle of soaking rains and drying sun often loosened the nails and lifted the nail heads above the surface of the boards. As a result, some builders turned to screws, which are more time consuming to install but eliminate the nail-popping problem.

Although nails and screws are functional, they're visible. In fact, pairs of nail or screw heads marching at 16 in. on center across a deck can be distracting. Countersinking the screw heads and filling the holes with plugs minimizes the problem but adds considerable time—and cost—to the installation. In response to this dilemma, a new method of attaching decking boards to the joists—hidden fasteners—is now in practice.

Hidden fasteners are "invisible" and are typically attached through the edges or bottoms of decking boards and the joists. There are many types of hidden fasteners and fastening systems, some of which are specifically designed for certain types of decking. Although hidden fasteners solve the visibility problem, they are considerably more expensive and take a lot more time to install than exposed nails and screws, adding significantly to the overall cost of the job. Some types may present other issues. Concealed fasteners may not secure the decking as tightly as face screws and can result in the decking moving or squeaking. In fact, some types are designed to allow the decking to move. This feature can also present another issue, the loss of the lateral bracing effect that screws provide. This can be addressed by adding additional bracing to the deck frame.

Hidden decking fasteners automatically provide a uniform spacing between decking boards, but when decking is installed with nails or screws, the space has to be set for each individual board. Many carpenters create gaps that are about $\frac{1}{8}$ in. wide. Debris collects in this narrow space, which is hard to clean and can lead to premature rot or decay. During the planning stages, discuss this issue with your builder and consider using a wider spacing, perhaps $\frac{3}{8}$ in., which should diminish this problem.

This redwood decking, a very stable wood, is firmly secured to the joists with decking screws. Choosing dark-colored screws and driving them just below the surface of the wood can make them appear less visible.

Sometimes it can feel like a crime to mar a beautiful, unblemished decking surface by puncturing it with nails or screws. If you find yourself getting a little squeamish at the thought, consider using one of the hidden fastening systems.

Railings

Railings are a prominent deck feature, so it's important to pay careful attention to their style and detailing. They create a horizontal element that can visually tie together a complicated deck plan, add some spice to an otherwise blank building facade, or break up the looming wall of a very tall house. They also create a sense of dynamic, linear movement, which can be accentuated by certain types of railings, such as wire cables. Other railing styles syncopate that motion by employing a rhythmic combination of thick posts and thin balusters.

Because they are so visible, railings go a long way toward expressing the style of the entire deck and its relationship with your house. If your house is traditional, for example, you could choose a matching railing style or be daring and add some playful elements. A simple house could benefit from a dressed-up railing or, perhaps, one with a rustic design.

Another design decision is the relationship between the railing and the decking, and you have the option of matching or contrasting the two. For example, a wooden railing constructed and finished the same way as the decking minimizes the visual distinction between the two. Manufacturers of synthetic decking offer matching railing systems to create a coordinated look. Modern-looking cables, because they tend to "disappear" when installed in wooden or synthetic posts, blend in with the decking. Alternately, a railing system that uses metal posts and balusters introduces a contrasting element, but because their profiles are relatively small, the difference is usually pleasing rather than jarring.

Simple rail caps not only dress up the top of a post, creating crisp, clean lines, but they also protect the vulnerable end grain, which, when left unprotected, can suck up water like a straw, leaving the post susceptible to rot.

Railing Code Requirements

Local building codes typically specify under what conditions decks must have railings as well as the specific dimensions and tolerances that are required. Always check with your local building official to make sure your railing will be in compliance.

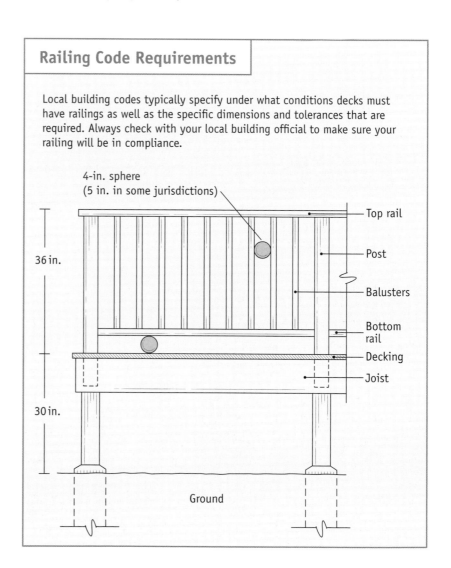

4-in. sphere
(5 in. in some jurisdictions)

Top rail

Post

Balusters

Bottom rail

Decking

Joist

36 in.

30 in.

Ground

right • This simple X design offers a pleasing respite from the typical vertical baluster. When creating unusual designs, be sure they meet all code requirements.

below • Interrupting the regular baluster pattern with another design can be an effective way to spice up a railing.

SAFETY REQUIREMENTS

Design aside, the purpose of a railing is to keep people safe. Even though you may not want one on your deck, many building codes require railings on decks that are 30 in. or more above the ground.

A code-prescribed railing is typically 36 in. high, but for added safety, some situations—if you have active children or a very high deck, for example—might call for 42-in.-high railings. Check code requirements with your local building inspector.

The typical railing system consists of four parts—posts, top rails, bottom rails, and balusters. The posts, usually constructed of 4x4s, do the lion's share of the work, providing much of the railing's strength. The top and bottom rails tie the posts together and also secure the balusters, the small vertical members that fill the spaces between the posts.

There are numerous variations to the basic railing. For example, some railings omit the balusters and replace them with horizontal boards, plastic-coated steel cables, or even sheets of clear plastic. There are some concerns to keep in mind when selecting an alternative-style railing system, as they may put children or wildlife at risk. A railing with horizontal boards can look like a playground ladder to young children who might climb them and risk injury. Check with the local building inspector and codes before installing them, or avoid the idea of them if you have young children in your family. Clear glass or plastic panels used in place of balusters have proven to be problematic for birds, who may not see them and collide with them, causing injury or death. Keep this possibility in mind before choosing this type of railing system.

Just as with decking, railings can be constructed with a number of materials, including wood, metal, wood-plastic composites, and solid plastic, or a combination of one or more. Due to their relative strengths, some materials must have larger cross sections than others (wood versus metal, for example) to perform up to code. This additional bulk also adds visual weight to a railing, an effect you may not want.

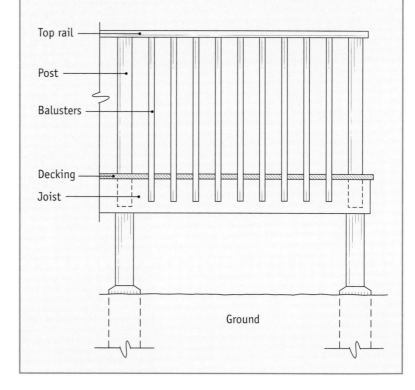

Safer Balusters

A common approach to installing balusters is to attach them directly to the floor or band joists. However, this method may result in the balusters not being strong enough to meet code requirements. Also, moisture can be trapped, which can lead to rot, decay, and ultimately baluster failure. Attaching balusters to a bottom rail that's designed to shed or drain water is a better option because it's stronger and longer lasting. And, from a mundane perspective, leaves and debris are easier to sweep under a bottom rail than between narrowly spaced balusters.

Top rail

Post

Balusters

Decking

Joist

Ground

above and right · The paneled posts, detailed caps, and closely spaced balusters lend a stately air to this gently curving railing. The top rail, made with the same material as the decking, ties the railing to the deck.

Types of Railings

You can custom-build railings on-site from individually purchased pieces, or you can install one of the many prefabricated railing systems that are available from a number of manufacturers. Railings have similar characteristics as decking made of the same material.

ALL WOOD
$-$$$

- The most common, typical deck railing type
- Materials are readily available
- Can be modified to fit any deck
- Construction method important—avoid water-trapping details
- Needs regular maintenance

METAL—IRON, STEEL, AND ALUMINUM
$$-$$$

- Stronger than wood—can use members with smaller cross sections
- May need to be constructed in a welding shop
- Painted steel and iron can rust and will need to be refinished
- Powder-coated aluminum has a long-lasting finish and will not rust
- May not be appropriate for all architectural styles

WOOD/SYNTHETIC AND METAL COMBINATIONS
$$-$$$

- Usually made with wood or synthetic rails and posts and metal balusters
- Combine the look of wood and the strength of metal
- Can be constructed on-site
- Thinner metal balusters are less visible than wood
- Need regular maintenance

POLYVINYL CHLORIDE (PVC) AND OTHER PLASTICS
$$

- Available in a number of styles
- Limited colors
- May not look very much like wood, particularly up close
- Durable and needs little maintenance
- Not as strong as wood but is reinforced with wood or metal inserts or with admixtures

WOOD-RESIN COMPOSITES
$$

- Look more like wood than vinyl
- Typically made from wood fiber and virgin or recycled plastic
- Manufacturers may offer matching decking boards
- Many utilize hidden fastening systems
- May be able to be shaped into curves
- Posts are typically sleeves that slide over wooden posts
- Modular systems may limit installation options

URETHANE FOAM
$$

- Looks, feels, and "works" the most like wood
- Available in a wide range of styles
- To protect it from UV rays, it comes primed and must be painted
- Because urethane is stable, paint should last longer than on wood

WIRE CABLE SYSTEMS
$$$

- Thin-diameter cables don't obscure view
- Costlier than most railings
- May not be appropriate for all architectural styles
- Three-inch spacing between cables is recommended for safety
- Posts, which can be wood or metal, may have to be closer together than with other systems

METAL SYSTEMS (ALUMINUM AND STEEL)
$$-$$$

- Smaller cross sections than wood or composite railings
- Have long-lasting, factory-applied finishes
- Many systems offer multiple options—balusters, glass panels, or cables—that work the posts and railings
- Modular systems may limit installation options

FIBERGLASS
$$-$$$

- Stronger than wood and synthetics, which allows smaller profiles
- Won't corrode or rust and is insect-resistant
- Comes in limited styles
- Colors are limited, although it can be painted

METAL

ALUMINUM

WIRE CABLE

Railings

Although decking boards can be installed in a number of patterns and designs, those choices seem limited when compared with the wide array of railing options. The different railing components—top and bottom rails, balusters (or their alternatives), and posts—when matched with the available railing materials—result in an almost infinite number of combinations and styles.

1. Colonial style balusters and railings are available in wood or synthetics and can be used to help a deck blend in with an existing porch railing. 2. This heavy-duty latticework extends up from the deck skirt to become part of the railing, but to avoid looking too busy, the handrail is supported by short balusters at just below eye level. The effect creates an interesting shadow pattern on the decking. 3. Although glass panels typically have a contemporary feel, they fit in beautifully with these traditionally styled posts.

4. Although two distinctly different materials were combined, the warmth of wood and the self-assurance of metal make for a happy marriage. As if to pay homage to its wood partner, every other aluminum baluster looks like it has been turned on a lathe. 5. A thin-gauge grid of plastic-coated wire makes for a simple but attractive baluster replacement. It's relatively inexpensive, easy to install, and visually unobtrusive. 6. Intermediate and significantly smaller posts provide additional horizontal support for the wire cables, divide spaces between the larger posts into restful squares, and set up an interesting thick/thin rhythm. 7. Contrasted with staid, white posts, these bowed metal balusters suggest playful movement and, when looked at as a group, create an interesting outline.

Stairs

All deck stairs are composed of three elements—treads, risers, and stringers. Handrails, like railings, are typically required by code when stairs rise more than 30 in. above the ground. Not only do stairs need to meet code requirements, but the stringers must be strong enough and the tread material stiff enough so that stairs feel solid underfoot.

COMPONENTS

Treads, the portion of the stairs that you step on, should be made from hard materials that can stand up to heavy traffic. They can be one solid piece or made from two separate boards. A **riser** is the board that spans the vertical distance between each tread. Sometimes riser boards are omitted. **Stringers** physically support the treads and provide nail backing for the risers. They are typically cut from a single piece of wood that's long enough to span the length of the steps. At a minimum, three stringers should be used for most steps, but more are usually required for steps that are wider than 4 ft.

During design and construction, a few other stair terms will likely be brought up: rise, total rise, run, and total run. Rise and run are units of measure, while treads and risers are physical components. Rise is a vertical measurement. A unit of rise is the height of a single step, and total rise is the distance from the bottom to the top of a set of steps. Run is a measure of horizontal distance. The unit of run is the depth of each step, and total run is the overall length of a set of steps.

As we move up and down stairs, we unconsciously become accustomed to the height between treads (rise). So when two sets of stairs are close to each other (such as between levels on a multilevel deck), it's important to keep the tread/riser configuration the same; otherwise, there's a risk of tripping.

Another stair concept you should know is pitch, a measure of steepness. Pitch is determined by the relationship of rise to run—the higher the rise and shorter the run, the steeper the stairs. Very steep stairs can be dangerous, so building codes prescribe the maximum and minimum rise and run dimensions.

above • The handrail and railing system match, along with their subtle color difference from the decking, makes these long stairs seem less overwhelming. Strategically placed, large planters at the foot of the stairs also soften the look of their steepness.

above • These wraparound steps offer unlimited access to the lawn and patio. Over time, if left unfinished, the wood will weather to a natural grey color, similar to the shingle siding.

left · Generously proportioned and stained the same color grey as the house and deck, this impressive set of stairs makes it easy to get to the landscape below and feels like a part of the deck rather than just a tacked-on appendage.

Typical Stair Components

As with railings, local building codes typically specify the dimensions and tolerances that are required for stairs. Always check with your local building official to make sure your structure will be in compliance.

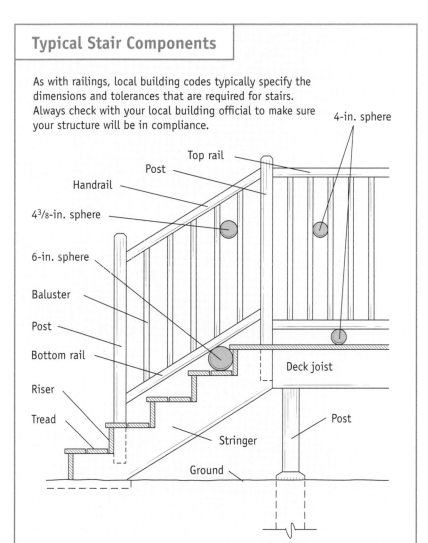

- 4-in. sphere
- Top rail
- Post
- Handrail
- 4³/₈-in. sphere
- 6-in. sphere
- Baluster
- Post
- Bottom rail
- Riser
- Tread
- Deck joist
- Stringer
- Post
- Ground

above · Near the bottom of this flight of steps, winder treads change the direction of travel. Like landings, winder treads are typically governed by building codes that detail the required dimensions.

DESIGN

In addition to their functional aspect, stairs are a design feature of a deck. This is true whether stairs connect one deck to another, lead from an on-grade or low-rise elevated deck to the ground, or stretch from a second-floor deck to the ground. There are some things you can do so that stairs are an integral and attractive part of your deck rather than a mere appendage.

Stair width is perhaps the most influential characteristic. The minimum width of stairs, as set by most building codes, is 3 ft., but in most situations this width is woefully inadequate for a deck. Set against the expanse of the great outdoors, a narrow flight of stairs can look downright wimpy, particularly if it is more than a few steps long. Three-foot-wide stairs don't allow two people to pass each other comfortably and can create a bottleneck. Lack of space for deck stairs is rarely an issue, so make them at least 4 ft. wide or even wider. Very wide stairs, particularly if they connect two decks, can create amphitheater-like seating and extra space for potted plants or sculpture.

To save money, it's not uncommon to build deck stairs with open risers. This approach reveals the rough-cut stringers, so unless you want a rustic look or plan to use a more finished-looking stringer system, consider closing the steps with riser boards, which make the stairs appear more substantial and hide hangers and fasteners, too. You can install the same decking material for the treads and risers or use contrasting materials. The sides of stringers are also visible. Again, to create a more finished look, cover them with the same material that's used for the treads and risers. To complete the look, countersink and plug exposed screws and bolts.

Stairs that begin at high-rise elevated decks and descend directly to the ground present specific challenges. As a general rule, because they are so long, it's best to locate these stairs off to the side of the deck rather than directly in front of the deck, where they can take up a lot of valuable space. This may mean they will have to double back to maintain a smaller footprint. Many codes require that stairs with a vertical rise of more than 12 ft. have an intermediate landing. Landings can be used as a place to turn stairs and can be enlarged to create a small deck.

The relatively thin profile of the top rail, which is the same tropical hardwood that's used for the decking, echoes the small diameter of the wire cables. The posts match the color of the riser boards, which, when paired with the railing and decking, makes for a nice two-tone effect.

above • A groove has been cut into the relatively thick face of this top rail, creating a thinner profile and making it easier to grip.

above • Serving both aesthetic and practical functions, two small decks break up the extremely long flight of steps that traverses this slope. They provide visual relief and, with their accompanying benches, places to rest. The upper deck is joined to the terraced garden via a stepping-stone path.

left • There's nothing quite as graceful as a curved stair. The beginning of this stair is marked with a double border that's a different color than the decking and stair treads but matches the posts and railings.

OUTFITTING

Furniture

Imagine proudly leading several of your close friends out onto your newly finished deck. What is the first thing that is likely to catch their eyes? The furniture! After all, the tables and chairs you'll need to fully enjoy your deck will cover up a lot of the decking and veil portions of the railing. First impressions mean a lot, so be sure that the furniture you choose reflects the same care and attention that you put into designing and building your deck.

Of course, choosing the right furniture goes beyond first impressions—you want to buy furniture that will last. The deck is an extension of your interior living space, so when furnishing it, consider buying outdoor furniture of the same quality as their indoor cousins. Actually, because outdoor furniture has to withstand a much harsher environment, invest in the highest quality your budget allows. Good quality furniture will enhance the visual appeal of your deck and reward you with years of service. Given the wide range of available materials—from wood and metal to wicker and synthetics—you might want to buy your furniture from a store with a knowledgeable sales staff that can answer your questions and provide informed advice.

above right • This built-in, furnished with refined white cushions and colorful accent pillows, looks more like a couch than a bench, which is normally associated with decks. Its sleek lines are in keeping with the adjacent and surrounding rooftop architecture.

right • Casual yet stylish, this dining set feels right at home on this simple on-grade deck. The glass-topped table is edged with wicker to match the chairs, and the umbrella can be lowered with a hand crank to welcome the sun.

When it comes to outdoor furniture, flexibility is a big plus. The cushion-topped ottomans can be used to prop up your feet or, in a pinch, as extra seats. Remove the cushions and you have a couple of handy side tables.

Things to Consider when Purchasing Outdoor Furniture

While the quality and type of material certainly go a long way in determining the life span of a piece of furniture, there are a number of other factors to consider, too.

- **Materials vs. nature.** Compare the weather conditions on your deck to how furniture materials stand up to those elements. For instance, on a very sunny deck, avoid having metal furniture sit in the sun's direct path, as some of it can get scorching hot. On the same sunny deck, if you decide you want metal furniture, plan for it to go in an area under an overhead structure.

- **Production quality.** Pay attention to the quality of the workmanship or manufacturing when shopping. Look for furniture with tight, solid joints, neat welds, and smooth edges. Inspect the finish. Paint and other coatings should be even and intact, without noticeable gaps or cracks. Hardware and screws should be rust-resistant and beefy enough to last for years.

- **Weight.** Furniture made of lightweight materials, such as aluminum and tubular steel, is easy to move, which makes rearrangement and storage less of a chore. When sitting, it's easier to push away from a table with a lightweight chair than with a heavier one. Keep in mind, however, that a gust of wind can also rearrange furniture and even send it tumbling off the edge of a deck or down the stairs, so plan accordingly.

- **Deck size.** Large, bulky furniture or furniture made from visually heavy materials, such as wood or composites, can overwhelm a small deck, particularly if there are many pieces to a set. On the other hand, furniture with a delicate profile can appear lost on a large deck.

- **Style.** Outdoor furniture is produced in a wide variety of styles from ornate to sleek and modern, so let the style of your home and deck inform your decision. Unless you want to make a strong statement with your furniture or you're trying to match a particular style, avoid heavy ornamentation and consider designs that express their beauty with clean, simple lines.

- **Ease of storage.** In most areas of the country, the coming of winter chases us off of our decks and into the warmth of our homes. To prolong the life of your deck furniture, it's a good idea to store it out of the harsh winter weather. Furniture that stacks or folds up will reduce the amount of storage space that's required.

- **Comfort.** Before you purchase a particular piece of furniture, it's imperative that you try it out first. Sit in chairs, recline in loungers, and pull a dining chair up to the table to make sure that you find the seat and the sitting position comfortable.

- **Cushions.** One way to increase the comfort of furniture with hard or rigid seats, such as wood, wicker, and metal, is to add cushions. There are cushions to satisfy every style preference and budget. Cushions come in a wide variety of sizes and can be two- or one-piece construction. Many are shaped to fit specific seat configurations. You can shop for ready-made cushions at large home and building centers or order custom-made ones from specialty shops. The cushion itself can be made from various materials such as poly-fiber fill or foam. Be sure to make sure the cushions you choose are rated for outdoor use. Cushion fabric is, of course, a great way to add color and pizzazz to your deck.

Types of Outdoor Furniture

Each type of furniture has its pluses and minuses that should be factored into the furniture-buying equation along with cost and style.

MOLDED PLASTIC
$

- Made from molded plastic resins
- Very lightweight
- Rated for outdoor use
- May degrade in the sun over time
- No maintenance is required

ALUMINUM
$–$$$

- Very lightweight, so may be blown by high winds
- Will not rust, but unprotected aluminum can oxidize and pit
- Painted aluminum will not oxidize but will need to be repainted to maintain finish
- Powder-coated finishes are tougher and last a lot longer than paint
- Most aluminum furniture has some type of fabric seat

PLANK PLASTIC
$$

- Made from individual pieces, or planks, similar to synthetic decking
- Can be made with either virgin or recycled plastic or a wood/plastic composite
- Attempts to imitate wood with varying degrees of success
- Comes in a variety of colors
- Rated for outdoor use
- No maintenance is required

WOOD
$$–$$$

- Has a natural beauty
- Stays cool in the sun
- Can be heavy, depending on the type of wood and construction
- To keep original appearance requires regular maintenance with paint, stain, or sealer
- Some woods are more rot-resistant than others, and all woods are vulnerable to rot at the joints and bottoms of the leg

STEEL
$$–$$$

- Strong and relatively lightweight
- With the exception of stainless steel, will rust unless painted
- Paint will crack and peel over time and need to be refinished
- Stainless steel has a "cool" modern look

NATURAL WICKER
$$–$$$

- Made from natural fibers, such as rattan
- Relatively lightweight
- Usually requires cushions to be comfortable
- Most is not rated for use in uncovered areas
- Painted wicker has to be repainted from time to time

SYNTHETIC WICKER
$$–$$$

- Made from materials such as vinyl resins
- May have an "unnatural" shine
- Relatively lightweight
- Rated for outdoor use, even in uncovered areas
- No maintenance is required

MIXED MATERIALS
$$–$$$

- Combines the desirable qualities of two or more materials
- Fabric seats with wood or metal frames may eliminate the need for cushions
- Depending on the type of materials used, may require maintenance
- The use of fabric makes heavy furniture look lighter

WROUGHT AND CAST IRON
$$$

- Very heavy
- Rated for outdoor use but will rust unless painted regularly
- Available with plastic coatings
- Can get hot in the direct sun

left · This set of high-quality wood furniture is lovely to look at, built to last, and comfortable, thanks to the cushions. Furniture arms also add to the level of comfort.

bottom left · Tucked into the corner of a seaside deck, this dining set of tightly woven wicker chairs and a wooden table takes full advantage of the view. The legs of the table are placed at 45 degrees to the seating positions so that they will not get in the way when the chairs are pulled up to the table.

below · The couch and two chairs all have curved fronts, which allow them to gather tightly around the round coffee table and encourage quiet conversation.

WOOD

Wood has been used for centuries to make furniture, and its timeless appeal and inherent beauty make it a natural choice for outdoor furniture. Wood can be tooled into lots of comfortable shapes, and when well finished and sanded smooth, it's inviting to sit in. Wood is not as conductive as other materials, such as metal, so when you first sit down you won't be shocked by a hot or cold seat. Depending on the piece, wood furniture can be heavy, but that heft makes it feel substantial.

The major challenge facing wood furniture is standing up to the elements. Rain can lead to rot and decay, and sun can cause wood to check, split, and warp. Choose furniture that is made from naturally rot-resistant, stable woods. For years, teak has been the preferred choice for high-quality wood furniture. Teak, like all tropical hardwoods, has naturally occurring oils and resins that fend off water and a dense, tight grain that resists splitting and warping.

Due to its popularity, however, teak has been overharvested, and now it's mostly grown on plantations that utilize faster-growing hybrid trees, which are not as strong or rot-resistant as the old-growth wood. In response, manufacturers use a number of other tropical and temperate hardwoods that have the same qualities as teak—ipé, balau, acacia, merbau, and jarrah—to make their furniture. Also available are several rot-resistant North American species of wood, including redwood, white cedar, red cedar, and cypress. Pressure-treated woods are another option. As with wood decking, many manufacturers use sustainably harvested wood to make their furniture. Check their websites or ask your retailer for specific information.

To paint or not to paint wood furniture is the question. Colorful furniture is a joy to behold, and high-quality, factory-applied finishes are long lasting. However, sooner or later the paint will chip or crack and will need to be refinished. Staining wood furniture is also an option. On the other hand, most tropical hardwoods do not accept paint or stain readily and are therefore sold "natural," or unfinished. When left to weather, these woods develop a soft, silvery grey color. While it is possible to apply finishing oils to maintain the wood's original color, you're setting yourself up for years of maintenance.

above • The gaps in the tops of wooden tables allow water to drain through and the boards to dry out between rains, but they can create an uneven surface upon which to place plates, glasses, and silverware. Rather than covering the entire surface with a tablecloth, using place mats lets the beauty of the wood still show through.

facing page top • Furniture doesn't always have to be arranged in elaborate groups. Located at a narrow end of the deck but just outside a door, this single wooden bench is large enough to comfortably accommodate three people but not so large that one person would feel lost.

left • Set against the white and grey background of the railing, deck, and house, this array of brightly painted wooden Adirondack chairs is soaking in the sun and view. One of the advantages of this style chair is that it has extra-wide arms that can double as petite side tables, great for setting down drinks and plates of food.

IRON

Historically, iron, both cast and wrought, was commonly used to make outdoor furniture and was the material of choice in the late 1800s. **Cast iron** is relatively brittle and requires the use of comparatively large cross sections to overcome this quality. As a result, cast-iron furniture is extremely heavy and more commonly used for furniture that's permanently installed, such as in parks and other public spaces. Cast-iron seats can feel lumpy and may not be the most comfortable option. If you're thinking about cast-iron furniture, keep both of these things in mind and be sure you try before you buy.

Wrought iron is very tough and more malleable than cast iron, so thinner components can be used. Although it is lighter and more portable than cast iron, wrought-iron furniture is still relatively heavy. True wrought iron is currently not produced in large quantities, and commercially available "wrought-iron" furniture is actually made from mild steel—iron to which a small quantity of carbon has been added.

Both cast and wrought iron will rust if exposed to the elements, so it must be painted. As an alternative to paint, some furniture manufacturers cover their metal furniture with a plastic coating or a powder coating (see "Aluminum" on the facing page). Although these factory-applied coatings are tough and long lasting, as with most coatings, weather will eventually take its toll and the furniture will have to be refinished.

Although not nearly as popular as it once was, cast-iron furniture still has its devotees. To minimize the problems caused by its weight, many cast-iron pieces, such as this set of table and chairs, are relatively small.

left · Improved manufacturing procedures and high-quality finishing techniques have turned aluminum furniture, such as these powder-coated table and chairs, from what was once regarded as a low-end, cheap product to something that's desirable and even sophisticated.

above · Outdoor furniture is available in a wide array of configurations suitable for almost any use or occasion. A bar-height bistro table and chairs elevate their occupants' eye level and point of view, permitting them to see over the tops of railings, bushes, or other obstacles.

ALUMINUM

Aluminum is lightweight and strong. Over the past several years, this unique combination has made it one of the most popular types of outdoor furniture materials. There are two types of aluminum used to make furniture—extruded and cast. Extruded aluminum is drawn through a die to create hollow tubes with round, oval, or rectangular cross sections. The first extruded aluminum furniture was inexpensive, with frames made from simple round tubes that were bolted together. Cast aluminum is made by pouring liquid aluminum into molds. This results in a solid product, which is heavier and feels more substantial than extruded aluminum but is still relatively lightweight. Cast-aluminum furniture is generally more expensive than extruded aluminum, and both are available in a wide range of styles.

Although aluminum doesn't rust like iron, it does oxidize and if unprotected will develop a white residue and may even pit, weakening the metal. Paint is widely used to protect extruded and cast aluminum, but in recent years another process, *powder coating*, has gained popularity. In this process, the powder is electrostatically applied to the surface of the metal and then heat-cured to form a skin. The resulting finish is tougher than conventional paint.

STEEL

Steel is iron that has been combined with varying amounts of carbon. Steel is stronger and heavier than aluminum but lighter than cast iron and wrought iron. Although steel outdoor furniture is not as common as other furniture, it has a niche market. Like iron and aluminum, most steel, with the exception of stainless, will rust when left outdoors unless protected with paint. Stainless steel has a very high carbon content and will not rust, making it perfect for those who want a bare steel look.

SYNTHETICS

In the never-ending struggle against the elements, furniture makers have turned to synthetic materials— plastics and wood/plastic composites—to address some of the shortcomings of wood and metal. There are two types of synthetic furniture—molded and plank.

Synthetic molded furniture is typically made from plastic resins in one piece. It's relatively light, inexpensive, and due to the popularity of the ubiquitous white tables and chairs, is probably the first thing that comes to mind when you think "plastic furniture." In fact, there's a certain honesty to molded plastic furniture—it doesn't try to be or look like something it's not.

Synthetic plank furniture is composed of multiple pieces. Synthetic planks are manufactured from either solid plastic or wood/plastic composites, in dimensions, shapes, and finishes intended to resemble wood boards. The rough planks are then cut to size and assembled with hardware, just like their wooden relatives. Furniture made from synthetic planks, particularly composite furniture, is heavier than molded plastic and, due to increased labor costs, more expensive. It comes in many styles, and some manufacturers do a better job than others of imitating painted wood.

Most plastic and composite furniture is made with recycled materials—typically plastic milk jugs and bottles. Synthetic furniture won't rot, crack, or splinter and is available in a virtual rainbow of colors. Because the color is an integral part of the material, it won't peel like paint. However, ultraviolet light can degrade synthetics—remember the chalky residue on those early white plastic chairs?—and the colors may fade over time. To combat this problem, manufacturers add ultraviolet light inhibitors to their raw material mixes.

Synthetic furniture doesn't have to be plain. These composite chairs have a stylish profile and are fitted with vinyl strapping and colorful seat cushions to make them more comfortable.

above • Molded plastic chairs are basic, to the point, serviceable, and stackable for easy storage. As with most things, you get what you pay for, so, given that molded plastic furniture is inexpensive to begin with, it makes sense to spend a bit more for higher-quality brands.

right • Not all molded plastic furniture is white, as these green chairs demonstrate. Although no one would mistake them for wood, the manufacturer was fairly successful in giving them a little more character than is typical.

WICKER

Wicker, or woven, furniture has a long history, and its use can be traced as far back as ancient Egypt. Historically, wicker furniture was made by weaving strands of any number of different types of natural plant materials into the desired form. Rattan, a vine that's a type of palm, was used extensively in the 1800s to make wicker furniture, which was extremely popular during the Victorian period. However, as tastes shifted to furniture with more clean-cut lines and people tired of the constant need to repaint it, wicker furniture fell out of favor.

Fueled partly by a nostalgic appreciation of earlier styles as well as the introduction of synthetic wicker, which greatly reduced the cost of production, wicker-style furniture experienced a resurgence that began in the 1970s and continues today. There are two basic types of synthetic wicker—paper-wrapped, high-strength wire wicker; and plastic, or resin, wicker. Unlike natural rattan, synthetic wicker must be supported by a sturdy frame to retain its shape.

All-weather wicker, which is rated for outdoor use, is available in all three types of materials, although resin wicker, because of its maintenance-free, rot-resistant characteristics, is often the preferred choice. Modern, factory-applied finishes have extended the life of and greatly reduced the need to refinish natural and paper-wrapped wicker furniture.

Wicker furniture is available in a number of colors, and for added comfort, it's often paired with seat and back cushions, which can add additional flair. As with all furniture, it's important to sit in wicker furniture before you make a purchase. Pay attention to the depth of the seat and the slope of the back and arms. Some folks find certain wicker weaves uncomfortable on their bare skin.

above • White is the traditional color for wicker furniture, and this set is a nice match for the white balusters and posts. The two-tiered side table offers a convenient place to store the service tray after the drinks have been passed around.

above • Although certainly attractive, these chairs might not be the best match for the table. Their arms are too high to slide under the table and, because the chair seats are very deep, it could be difficult to find a comfortable sitting position.

Wicker furniture is often associated with old-fashioned front porches, but today's wicker is designed to come out from under cover and into the open. These chairs and ottoman enjoy the view from a second-floor deck.

MIXED MATERIALS

Although a rugged metal chair may do a great job of standing up to the elements, it may not be the most comfortable to sit on. And while there's something to be said for the simple beauty of an all-wood table, sometimes you'd just like to jazz things up a bit. Mixed-material furniture can solve both dilemmas.

Mixed-material chairs and lounges are typically made with wood or metal frames over which some type of fabric is installed. Much of the early mixed-material furniture of the 1950s and 1960s, such as the canvas and wood and the plastic strapping and aluminum tubing folding furniture, was inexpensive and not very durable. The canvas rotted relatively quickly, and the thin aluminum frames bent easily. However, manufacturers now produce high-quality furniture with strong frames and rot-resistant fabrics. Sling furniture, with either wood or metal frames and plastic mesh seats and backs, are extremely comfortable and among the most popular type of mixed-material furniture. Seats and backs are also made from wicker, woven plastic straps, other outdoor-rated synthetic fabrics, and even cotton canvas.

Tables are made with multiple materials, too. Not long ago, glass was the material of choice for mixed-material tables, but a number of other materials, including plastic, marble, slate, tile, granite, and even polished concrete, have now found favor. Bases and tabletops can be wood, metal, or plastic.

above · **The contoured, high backs of these aluminum and mesh-fabric sling chairs offer great support and comfort, assuring that conversation will continue long after the meal is over. The cantilevered, sled-style legs give a slight spring to the chairs, making them even more comfortable.**

right · **These lightweight metal and mesh-fabric chairs are a snap to move and, when the spirit moves you, would be easy to carry into the gardens. They fold up for compact storage.**

left · Overstuffed furniture isn't just for the indoors any more. These metal frames have fabric-covered back supports and minimal seat slats, which have to be used with the integrated seat cushions.

below · Cushions are one way to make wood seats softer, but there is another—replace the seat and, while you're at it, the back with another material. The backs and seats of the chairs around the dining table are mesh, which makes them more comfortable, lighter, and quick drying after a rain.

Outdoor Electronics

As wonderful as it can be to enjoy nature from your deck, there might be times when you want to experience some inside entertainment outdoors. This can be as simple as drilling a few holes in a wall and wiring a couple of speakers up under the eaves or, since the world of outdoor electronics has changed dramatically, as intricate as installing entire audio and visual components—stereos, TVs, satellite receivers, and home theaters—outside. Many of these items can be located anywhere on your deck where there's a nearby power source and speaker wires can be easily hidden from view.

Weatherproof stereos and TVs are designed to be exposed to the elements and permanently installed outdoors. Their all-weather cases safeguard the electrical components against water, dust, dirt, and insects and can withstand direct exposure to ultraviolet light. Outdoor stereos and TVs can handle quick, large temperature swings and function in a wide range of temperatures, from below 0°F to above 100°F. To "fill" the openness of exterior space and overcome the inevitable background noise, outdoor TVs have more powerful speakers than their interior counterparts, and improved antiglare coatings to reduce veiling reflections. Both outdoor stereos and TVs can be attached to walls, installed on poles, placed inside fixed cabinetry, or set on portable furniture for more flexibility. A built-in ground-fault circuit interrupter (GFCI), which protects users from electric shock, is a desirable safety feature (and in some districts may even be required, so check your local codes). And choosing a waterproof, or at least weather-resistant, remote control is a plus.

For an open-air theater experience, you can buy an outdoor movie system. A typical system includes an inflatable movie screen, a projector, speakers, and required wires, cables, and connectors. These systems are much larger than TVs, with the viewing areas measured in feet (for example, 9 ft. wide and 5 ft. tall), not inches, and are great for keeping large gatherings entertained. Other electronic equipment, such as DVD players, audio mixers, and MP3 players, are also available.

The step-up, four-poster pergola and blank house wall make this a great place to grab a movie or ballgame while enjoying the sites and sounds of the outdoors. Lowering the TV so that it's at eye level would make it perfect.

Where to Put the TV

If you will incur the expense of outfitting your deck with a weatherproof TV, you should invest a little time in planning its location. The following guidelines will increase your outdoor viewing pleasure.

- Viewing height—TVs are commonly installed too far above the floor. Television screens are designed to display optimal color and brightness when viewed at the center of the screen. This means that when sitting, which is how most of us watch TV, the center of the screen should be at eye level. Tilting your head back to view an elevated TV can be uncomfortable and even result in a stiff neck. Lounge chairs, dining chairs, and stools are all different heights, so take that into account when you're determining TV placement. If your TV will be viewed from more than one type of chair, consider mounting it so it can easily be moved up and down.
- Viewing angle—Although manufacturers are continually making improvements, picture quality suffers when a TV is viewed off to the side. Some types and makes of TVs have larger viewing angles than others, so be sure to plan your TV-viewing seating so that everyone can see the screen clearly.
- Lines of site—It can be annoying to have your line of site to the TV continually disrupted. To avoid having people block your view, try to locate the TV in an out-of-the way corner, or position it so that they don't have to walk between the seating and TV screen to reach another part of the deck or get into the house.

above • Although cooking outdoors is enjoyable, the cleanup can still be a chore, even in a full-service outdoor kitchen. A TV takes a bit of the drudgery out of the cleanup task.

left • Music is a natural mood setter. Rig up some speakers on your deck to set the tone for social gatherings.

Fireplaces

The visual and emotional appeal of an open fire is irresistible. It pleases the senses and can allow you to enjoy your deck when chilly air might otherwise drive you inside. There are two basic types of exterior fire sources—freestanding fireplaces and fire pits—that can add charm and ambiance to your deck.

FREESTANDING FIREPLACES

Some freestanding outdoor fireplaces are designed to be installed on your deck. A popular type of outdoor fireplace is the chiminea, a small, Mexican-style fireplace that sports a round, chubby base and short chimney. Chimineas are traditionally made of clay, but cast-iron versions are available. Although heavier than fire pits (see pp. 180–181), chimineas and other small fireplaces can be moved.

Large outdoor fireplaces that more closely resemble interior fireplaces are another option. These, too, come in many styles, materials, and finishes. They are typically sold in kits that stack and bolt together and can be quickly assembled by one or two people. Heavier than chimineas, freestanding fireplaces, unless they are disassembled, cannot be easily moved. Some fireplaces can be set up for cooking or even baking. How does pizza al fresco sound?

above · Discretely positioned in a remove corner, this chiminea stands ready, waiting to ward off the chill. When in use the chairs can be pulled up close to take full advantage of the warming flames.

right · The outside hearth of this massive fieldstone fireplace and chimney looks out past the exposed aggregate patio and onto the adjacent deck. Large rocks, which also serve as permanent seating, extend into the deck, visually and physically linking the fireplace, patio, and deck.

Fire Safety

Although fireplaces can be a wonderful addition to a deck, there is a certain amount of inherent danger with any open flame. Therefore, it is extremely important to implement fire safety.

- Before purchasing a fireplace or other heat source, check with your local building inspector or fire safety official to learn about any codes or regulations governing their installation or use.
- Maintain code-required and manufacturer-suggested clearance around and underneath a fireplace.
- Most decking and deck framing is flammable, so install a fireproof mat under and on the area surrounding a fireplace.
- Keep the area around a fireplace clear of clutter and flammable materials.
- Permanently install a fire extinguisher near the fireplace.
- Never locate anything that uses an open flame under a low-hanging tree or roof overhang.
- Never leave a fire unattended.
- Be sure the fire is completely out before leaving the fireplace.

A raised hearth lifts the fire up off the ground and places it closer to the eye level of those sitting around it. The hearth can also be used as a seat to really cozy up to the fire.

FIRE PITS

A "fire pit" might be a bit of a misnomer when it's associated with decks. Instead of being dug into the ground, as the name suggests, many deck fire pits are freestanding bowls or pots that are raised above the deck's surface on legs. Usually constructed of copper, cast iron, or steel, raised fire pits are available in a wide range of styles, shapes, and finishes. Small fire pits are portable and can be moved to different locations as weather conditions or the time of day requires. Some fire pits come with accessories that allow them to double as grills. A variation of the fire pit is a fire-pit table, which has a table surface that surrounds the fire pit. Fire-pit tables are available in coffee table or dining table heights. When designed to cook food, you can prepare your meal and eat it without having to move.

Fire pits and fireplaces are available as solid-fuel burning (such as wood) or gas burning (either natural gas or propane). Gas-burning fire pits and fireplaces are a good option if you're worried about stray embers and may be required by code in some areas. Natural gas models must be permanently connected directly to a fixed gas line, whereas portable propane models offer a measure of flexibility.

Carved out of solid stone, this stunning fire pit is integrated with the top of the stone and concrete bench that glides along the edge of the deck. Planters of the same shape, size, and material enhance the composition and mark the steps that lead to the patio.

above · This wicker seating set includes a matching fire pit table. The metal fire pit is installed off-center in the glass top, which creates more usable space for setting down plates and glasses.

top left · Located at the opposite end of the deck as the outdoor kitchen, with the dining table in between them, this raised fire pit is designed to be a focal point for the after-dinner conversation.

bottom left · Echoing the shape of the raised fire pit, the stone bench that encloses it does double duty as a retaining wall, holding back the hillside. A round hearth completes the circle and keeps the wooden deck a safe distance from any wayward embers.

Outdoor Heaters

Although not as romantic as fireplaces, outdoor heaters certainly have their place. Their sole purpose is to produce heat, which they do efficiently. There are several types of outdoor heaters, including freestanding, tabletop, wall, ceiling, and pole-mounted models. Hanging patio heaters and "under umbrella" models are also available. Freestanding heaters often come with wheels to make moving them easier. In addition to conventional convection heating, some heaters utilize radiant, or infrared, heat. These are more efficient types of heaters because, instead of warming the air, which can quickly disperse outdoors, they warm only the people and objects within their reach.

above • The narrow profile of this heater allows it to be tucked up under the rafters and against the beam.

facing page • Strategically located in an out-of-the-way corner, this propane heater will generate plenty of heat to ward off the chilly air and keep the diners comfortable.

Types of Outdoor Heaters

If you want to feel comfortable after the sun goes down and chilly air settles in but don't want to put up with the hassle of tending fire, then an outdoor heater may be the answer. These heaters use natural gas, propane, or electricity. There are several options to choose from, so take some time to think about which would work best for your situation.

TABLETOP
$
- Small heaters intended to heat small seating groups
- Propane and butane models can be located anywhere; electric models require access to power
- Some models offer adapters for 5-gal. liquefied petroleum (LP) tanks
- Some electric models resemble table lamps

HANGING
$
- Relatively small and intended for small areas
- Can be used in a series for additional heat and an interesting effect
- Most residential models use electricity, but gas and LP units are available
- Wires can be concealed in overhead structures

MOUNTED
$$
- Units are typically fastened to walls, ceilings, or poles
- Some types can be attached to movable, tripod-style poles
- Most residential models use electricity, but gas and LP units are available
- Due to their permanent installation, careful placement is a must

FREESTANDING
$$–$$$
- Tall units that direct their heat downward
- Propane models can be located anywhere
- Natural gas and electric models need a hook-up nearby
- Some models have wheels for easy moving

Water Features

Humans seem to have an undeniable attraction to water, and water has an intrinsic, primordial hold over us. Like all creatures, we have a need to be near water, and most early civilizations developed close to water. We can spend hours looking out over the ocean, listening to the waves crash ashore; become contemplative while staring into a clear, deep pool of water; and be mesmerized by a rushing stream, as it laughs and gurgles its way over rocks. Water has a soothing, even healing, effect on us, so if you find yourself wanting to add a water feature to your deck, it's only natural.

Fountains and waterfalls are the two most common types of water features, and either can easily be added to a deck. Portable, self-contained models are available in many styles and can be set up virtually anywhere there's a level surface on a deck. However, when considering how to incorporate a water feature, keep in mind that a fountain or waterfall doesn't have to sit directly on the deck. Installing a water feature on the lawn adjacent to the deck is also a possibility. And while prefabricated units will work here, too, installing a custom-made feature offers more flexibility and the chance to explore your creativity. With more space, an artificial stream or reflecting pool become feasible options.

Water walls and bubble panels are two other water features to consider. Water walls, a type of waterfall, consist of vertical panels, typically glass, stone, or metal, that water is poured over. To enhance the effect, the panels are sometimes textured or shaped. Bubble panels are composed of two panels of glass that have water sandwiched between them. Air is introduced at the bottom of the panel and causes bubbles to form and travel up through the water in random and intriguing patterns.

As you walk from the patio down the steps to the deck, you are accompanied by a slow trickle of water as it makes its way from the top to the bottom of this low-rise water feature. Once seated, you can enjoy the sight and sound of the water as it continues on its journey.

above · It's said that you can't get water from a stone, but that doesn't seem to be the case here as water bubbles up from the middle of this rectangular rock and down over the sides. The rough-hewn sides create interesting patterns as the water slithers to the pebbles below.

top left · Apparently even a gentle spray of water has hypnotic powers. These chairs turn their backs on the distant view to focus their attention on the small geyser that springs from a spiral in the concrete walkway.

bottom left · A bit of ingenuity turned what would have been a conspicuous eyesore into a fascinating feature. Barely noticeable, a rain chain replaces a solid downspout and shepherds the rainwater from the gutter down through the deck.

Decorating with Plants

Adding plants to your deck is a great way to introduce stunning visual elements, movement, and fragrance to your outdoor living space. But before you run out to your local nursery, take a minute to mull things over. Taking care of plants can be a lot of work, so be sure you're ready to sign on for the long haul. It might make sense to start small, with a few select plants, before you make an extensive and expensive commitment. Plants can be placed on or around a deck—and you may very well want to utilize both of these options.

Plan your plantings much as you do your deck. Evaluate the site. Does it have partial or full sun, shade, or a mix of both? Is the climate dry or wet? Is it windy? Next, do a planting layout. Which are the areas on your deck that seem a little bare and could use some color? Do you want to screen the area underneath your deck? From which places on your deck or in your house do you want to see the plants? Either sketch out potential planting beds or outline them on the ground, or outline or place containers in different spots on your deck.

Once you have a good idea of where the plants will be located, create a list of possible plants and create a planting plan. If you're not familiar with the different types of plants, take an educational field trip to a local nursery. Wander around, look at informational tags, take some photos, and ask questions. As you choose plants and compile your list, it's helpful to have a unifying theme—for example, a particular flower or foliage color, plant species, or shape—and then introduce a few variations—some contrasting colors and different plant heights or plant structures. By limiting variety, you reduce the risk that your plantings will be a confusing jumble.

As you choose each plant, locate it on your planting plan. Like all design processes, you will choose and eliminate different plants, and revise your ideas more than once. Even after you've made your final choices, you will probably rearrange the location of a plant, shifting it until it's just right. But don't worry; as a master gardener once told me, if you don't like where you put a plant, just take it out and move it.

Choosing Plants

Choosing plants can be a daunting task. Here are some guidelines to help you through the process.

- Select plants that don't need a lot of maintenance, such as watering, pruning, or spraying.
- Consider native plants. They will fit well with the landscape, grow well in the climate, and are usually disease-resistant.
- Match your plants' needs to the amount of sun or shade around your deck.
- Pick plants that are appropriate in scale for their location and will remain that way over time.
- Choose plants that attract butterflies, hummingbirds, and other birds and wildlife.
- Select plants that have blooms and foliage that appeal to you, not because they're priced right or are the current rage.
- Choose plants that either bloom or hold their beauty for a long time.

above · A single pot will feel less isolated if it's put close to another deck feature, such as a post, stair opening, or level change, because in tandem each becomes more significant. A container raised on feet, like this one, will also keep moisture from getting trapped underneath it and causing wood decking to rot.

top left · A profusion of foliage seems to lift the ground up several feet, making this low-rise elevated deck appear to be almost on-grade. The nice mix of specimens includes some high, low, and even climbing varieties.

bottom left · Whether clustered together in large groupings or placed in pairs or individually, the timeless red clay pot is right at home on a deck. Using pots of varying sizes, shapes, patterns, and shades of red will eliminate any potential for them to be monotonous.

CONTAINER GARDENS

Perhaps the simplest way to introduce plants to your deck is by placing containers on it. Potted or container plants can be located almost anywhere—set on plant stands, hung from railings, or placed so they're marching up a flight of steps. Planters are larger containers than pots and, as we saw in chapter 3, are sometimes built in to the deck. There are many commercially available portable planters that may suit your taste, and sometimes they even come equipped with wheels so they can be moved as the spirit moves.

Other ways to bring plants onto your deck include window and railing boxes and hanging baskets. Baskets can be hung from arbors and pergolas and from brackets attached to walls or posts. In addition to purchasing boxes and baskets, you might rummage through your garage and turn something that's been discarded into a one-of-a-kind container. And don't limit yourself to just flowers. Practically anything that can be grown in a garden, such as herbs, fruits, and vegetables, can be grown in containers.

Gardening in a planter filled with soil can feel similar to working in a garden. Although it's certainly possible to place the soil directly against the sides of the planter, even the most rot-resistant wood will decay over time unless the inside of the planter is constructed with pressure-treated wood. A better approach is to use a synthetic planter or line a wooden planter with either a premade plastic liner or heavy-duty, waterproof material such as swimming pool liner or roofing material. This is particularly true if you will be planting vegetables because the chemicals from pressure-treated wood may leach into the soil.

Aligned along the length of the deck, a single row of planters forms a low wall of foliage that softens the wood-sheathed wall behind them. Each container holds the same mix of plants, but rather than being boring, it creates a pleasing rhythm and enhances the effect of creating a living wall.

above • All of these pots, some of which are on and hidden by the wooden bench, contain the same type of flowers. However, because there is enough variation in the size and orientation of the foliage and blooms, their similarity works as a unifying theme rather than being repetitive.

above • With potted plants, prickly roses, and a low planting bed, there's a little something for every taste here, but rather than feel overwhelming, it works. Although it may not appear so at first glance, it's organized—the potted plants are grouped together and flank the door; the roses climb the house and wall and pop up out of the bed; and the bed is populated mainly by a single plant.

If your planter is deeper than the depth needed for your plants to grow successfully, you can fill the bottom with rocks or build a false bottom at the depth you need. For example, if your planter is 12 in. deep but your plants only need 5 in. of soil to grow successfully, you can install the false bottom 7 in. from the actual bottom.

For all containers, make sure they're designed, or placed on the deck, with adequate ventilation space underneath them so that any water and moisture that finds it way there can be wiped up or will dry up in the breeze.

You can also use smaller containers inside of your planters. Among the advantages of doing so is you can quickly swap out plants with the changing seasons without having to dig up your existing beds and planting anew. You can also continually add new flowering plants to update your outdoor decor, and, of course, you can give your houseplants a "summer vacation" by moving them outdoors. Depending on the size of the plants, their pots can be quite large and vary in height, so be sure to keep that in mind when designing built-in, or buying manufactured, planters.

above • Symmetrically planted, this hanging railing basket is perfectly placed—centered between the railing posts and on the door behind it.

below • A potpourri of pots—some placed on the deck, others on the ground—enlivens this simple deck. The rustic window box, overhanging wisteria, and taller pine extend the greenery upward, adding a vertical dimension to the scene.

ARBORS AND TRELLISES

The shade, privacy, and sense of place that's created by well-positioned arbors and trellises are enhanced with the addition of plants such as climbing roses, ivies, Virginia creeper, and clematis. Some plants, such as wisteria, are beautiful but very aggressive growers and need regular pruning to be kept under control. Plants can be heavy, so make sure that your trellis or arbor is strong enough to support the additional weight.

Growing plants up a trellis on a deck is a good way to decorate a plain exterior wall or to add plants to a small deck without taking up a lot of space. Arbors can be placed at strategic locations to signify a transition to a different area of a deck, or they can be large enough to span an entire area of a deck, creating shade and privacy.

above left · A vine-covered trellis is one type of sun-control measure that automatically changes with the seasons. Metal is an excellent trellis material. It can be welded, bolted, or bent into any number of configurations and, due to its inherent strength, requires relatively small cross-sectional pieces to do the job.

left and below · When leafed out and in full bloom, this rose animates and adds color to the grey-shingled wall it's climbing. The Adirondack chairs are in an ideal spot to benefit from the cascading fragrance. A wooden trellis attached to the wall prevents the rose from damaging the shingles and offers the appropriate type of surface for climbing. The rose is planted in a rectangular planter that is inconspicuously flush with the surface of the deck.

AROUND THE DECK

Even though much of your focus has been trained squarely on the deck itself, don't forget the surrounding lawn and landscape when it comes to plants. When considering adding new plants to your landscape, it can be helpful to begin close to your deck and then work out farther into the yard.

Plants located close to a deck are typically planted in beds that are separated from the lawn by some type of border, edging, or sharp edge cut in the lawn. Planting beds create a transitional element between the deck and lawn and can visually soften a deck's hard edges. They can be virtually any shape and size you desire and can be extended into the lawn or along the sides of a walkway. Plants nearest the deck can be used in place of deck skirting, and those that keep their foliage can do the job year-round.

When selecting plants for on-grade patios, be sure to choose varieties that will not grow so high that over time they will block your view. And remember, much of the time you spend on a deck is spent seated, so keep that lower eye level in mind. On the other hand, tall plants can lessen the impact of and bring a sense of scale to taller elevated decks. It's also important to keep in mind that plants, particularly bushes and shrubs, grow out as well as up. Be sure to allow adequate space between the deck and the plants to accommodate the mature plant.

Now that you will be spending more time outdoors, you might want to enhance your views by adding some additional plantings to your yard. You could add a miniature "grove" of flowering fruit trees, screen an unsightly neighbor's fence with a row of bushes, or make an inviting oasis by planting an array of flowers around a simple bench. And plantings can be a great way to create a sense of soothing privacy around a pool, hot tub, or remote deck.

This beautiful border designates the main artery from the deck to the other parts of the property. The robust greens create a nice contrast with the orange parts of the house.

above · The narrow decking and the two chairs tucked into the corner indicate that this is a private area of the deck. The plants around it provide screening and serenity.

top left · After a season of fertilizing, watering, liming, and mowing your lawn, are you tired of all the expense and effort and perhaps dream about turning your lawn into something else? How about a field of flowers? True, flowers and plants also require work, but when you relax on your deck, you'll be rewarded with a colorful, ever-changing view.

above · Encouraged to climb on and above the railing, these roses form a fragrant privacy screen. A collection of shorter potted roses fill in the gaps below the railing.

Home outside the Home

When the owners purchased this home, it had everything they had wished for, with one major exception. Although the interior suited their needs to a tee, the outside was another matter. The back door opened to the yard—an empty yard. There was no defined space where they could sit and enjoy their sun-filled surroundings. In retrospect, that void was a blessing in disguise because, given a blank canvas, they were able to create a space that worked to suit their outdoor living needs. It didn't hurt that one of the owners was a professional builder specializing in decks and patios.

The couple's wish list was long, and rightly so, because the local climate permits outdoor living much of the year. Fond of entertaining, they realized that they wanted a place to do it all—cook, dine, sit, and relax—and determined that a deck would be the most effective way to create this extension of their interior space.

Most construction projects present a challenge or two, and this one was no exception. To shelter the deck from the sometimes-searing sun, a cover was added to the plans. However, to make the cover work with the house's roofline, the deck had to be shifted a few feet to the side. Zoning regulations also came into play. To fall within the setback limits, the deck had to be shortened slightly. However, this actually turned out to be a plus because the smaller deck feels cozier than a larger one would have.

above right • When viewed from the yard, the deck seems to be relatively small, but looks can sometimes be deceiving. There's a lot of usable space packed under the cover and behind the tightly spaced balusters.

right • The masonry planter that marks the entry to the steps cascades down its entire length. The wall-mounted lights illuminate the steps and plants.

left · The cover shelters a generous dining area, which has room for additional seating, including a built-in bench. The cover also provides a place to attach the curtain rods, which make it easy to hang and draw the curtains to create privacy or filter the low-angle sun.

bottom left · A full-service, U-shaped kitchen, which includes a service counter, built-in grill, sink, dishwasher, and wine cooler, is located on the open-air portion of the deck. The pergola shields the chef, who gets plenty of heat standing near the grill, from the sun.

below · Ending a built-in bench against something solid makes it appear more substantial and fixed in place.

Professional Organizations

AMERICAN INSTITUTE OF ARCHITECTS (AIA)
202-626-7300 or 800-242-3837
www.aia.org
Lists AIA member architects that specialize in residential work

AMERICAN INSTITUTE OF BUILDING DESIGN (AIBD)
800-366-2423
www.aibd.org
Provides professional certification and member referrals

AMERICAN SOCIETY OF LANDSCAPE ARCHITECTS (ASLA)
202-898-2444
www.asla.org
Information about landscape architecture

NATIONAL ASSOCIATION OF HOME BUILDERS (NAHB)
800-368-5242
www.nahb.org
Remodeling information for homeowners

NATIONAL ASSOCIATION OF THE REMODELING INDUSTRY (NARI)
800-611-6274
www.nari.org
Remodeling information for homeowners

NATIONAL OUTDOOR KITCHEN & FIREPLACE ASSOCIATION
888-838-8272
www.nokfa.org
Information on outdoor products and manufacturers

Manufacturer Associations

ASSOCIATION OF POOL & SPA PROFESSIONALS (APSP)
703-838-0083
www.apsp.org
Information about pools and spas and lists of installers

DECK INDUSTRY ASSOCIATION
www.deckindustry.org
Information about deck construction; lists deck builders and materials manufacturers and dealers

HEARTH, PATIO & BARBECUE ASSOCIATION
703-522-0086
www.hpba.org
Information on outdoor cooking and heating equipment; lists manufacturers and suppliers

NORTH AMERICAN DECK AND RAILING ASSOCIATION (NADRA)
888-623-7248
www.nadra.org
Information about deck construction; lists deck builders and materials manufacturers and dealers

Decking and Railing Manufacturers and Builders

ADVANTAGE™ TRIM & LUMBER
877-232-3915
www.advantagelumber.com
Wholesale and retail supplier of tropical wood lumber

ARCHADECK®
804-353-6999
www.archadeck.com
Custom deck design and construction

BACKYARD AMERICA™
877-489-8064
www.backyardamerica.com
Builder, manufacturer, and supplier of decks, railings, pergolas, and other outdoor structures

BISON INNOVATIVE PRODUCTS
800-333-4234
www.bisonip.com
Manufacturer of wood tiles and pedestal supports for rooftop and on-grade decking

DECKORATORS®
800-332-5724
www.deckorators.com
Manufacturer of metal and synthetic railing systems

FEENEY® ARCHITECTURAL PRODUCTS
800-888-2418
www.feeneyarchitectural.com
Manufacturer of cable railing systems

GARDENSTRUCTURE.COM
888-293-8938
www.gardenstructure.com
Designer, builder, and franchiser of decks, pergolas, and outdoor woodwork throughout North America

TREX®
800-289-8739
www.trex.com
Manufacturer of synthetic decking and railing systems

Manufacturers and Suppliers of Furniture, Equipment, and Accessories

KALAMAZOO™ OUTDOOR GOURMET
800-868-1699
www.kalamazoogourmet.com
Manufacturer of outdoor kitchen equipment

O.W. LEE CO.
909-947-3771
www.owlee.com
Manufacturer of outdoor furniture, fire pits, and accessories

TELESCOPE CASUAL FURNITURE
800-451-0938
www.telescopecasual.com
Manufacturer of outdoor furniture and accessories

Internet Resources

BUILDINGGREEN, INC.
www.buildinggreen.com/
Independent organization that provides green building product information and publications

ENERGY STAR
www.energystar.gov
Information on energy-efficient building and landscaping materials and techniques

U.S. ENVIRONMENTAL PROTECTION AGENCY
www.epa.gov/
Information on a wide range of consumer environmental and health concerns

Computer-Aided Design Programs

CHIEF ARCHITECT® HOME DESIGNER LANDSCAPE AND DECK 10
By Chief Architect

SKETCHUP™
By Google

TOTAL 3D™ HOME LANDSCAPE & DECK PREMIUM SUITE
By Individual Software

CREDITS

p. i: Photo © Rob Karosis, Architect: Rob Whitten, Whitten Architects, Portland, ME www.whittenarchitects. com

p. ii: Photo © Rob Karosis, Architect: Rob Whitten, Whitten Architects, Portland, ME www.whittenarchitects. com

p. iv: (1) Photo © Eric Roth; (2) Picture supplied by AdvantageLumber. com; (3) Photo courtesy www. GardenStructure.com; (4) Photo © Cesar Rubio, Design: Peter Pfau, AIA, Pfau Architecture Ltd., pfauarchitecture.com; (5) Photo by Matthew Borkoski, Courtesy of Trex (CK)

p. v: (1) Photo © Eric Roth; (2) Photo © Art Gray; (3) © 2005 Bison Innovative Products/www.BisonIP.com; (4) Photo © Allan Mandell, Design: Linda Ernst; (5) Photo by Matthew Borkoski, Courtesy of Trex (CK)

p. 1: Photo © Mark Lohman

p. 2: Photo © Olson Photographic LLC, Design: Four Square Builders

p. 4: (1) Photo © Rob Karosis, Architect: Sam Van Dam, Van Dam Architecture & Design, Portland, ME www.vandamdesign.com; (2) Photo: Steve Aitken, courtesy Fine Gardening, © The Taunton Press, Inc.; (3) Photo © www. kenricephoto.com; (4) Photo © davidduncanlivingston.com; (5) Photo © Greg Hursley; (bottom) Photo © Eric Roth

CHAPTER 1

p. 6: Eric Roth, Design: www. greencos.com

p. 8: (top) www.carolynbates. com; Design: Michael Dugan, AIA, Construction: Tom Sheppard, Sheppard Custom Homes (bottom): www.tonysears.com

p. 9: Erik Kvalsvik, Architect: Charles Warren, www.charleswarren.com

p. 10: Photo: Image provided by Archadeck®, America's outdoor living expert. www.Archadeck.com

p. 11: (top) Photo: Image provided by Archadeck®, America's outdoor living expert. www.Archadeck.com; (bottom) Eric Roth

p. 12: (top) Rob Karosis (bottom) Photo by Matthew Borkoski, Courtesy of Trex (CK)

p. 14: (top) Photo courtesy Dacor (bottom) Photo courtesy Richard McPherson, Landscape Architect, San Francisco

p. 15: Photo: Image provided by Archadeck®, America's outdoor living expert. www.Archadeck.com

p. 16: (photo 1) © Lee Anne White, Design: Simply Outdoorz, (photo 2) Photo courtesy Kalamazoo Outdoor Gourmet (photo 3) © Mark Lohman

p. 17: (photos 4, 5, & 7) Photos courtesy Kalamazoo Outdoor Gourmet; (photo 6) Photo © Tria Giovan Photography

p. 18: Photo © Philip Beaurline

p. 19: Photo © Linda Oyama Bryan for Van Zelst, Inc.

pp. 20-21: Lee Anne White

p. 22: (top) Photo courtesy the Association of Pool and Spa Professionals; (bottom) Archadeck

p. 23: Photo by Matthew Borkoski, Courtesy of Trex (CK), Design: Victoria Lister Carley

p. 24: Photo courtesy www. GardenStructure.com

p. 25: (top & bottom right) Photos: Images provided by Archadeck®, America's outdoor living expert. www. Archadeck.com; (bottom left) Photo © Rob Karosis, Design: Myke Hodgins, Hodgins and Associates Landscape Architects

pp. 26-27: Pictures supplied by AdvantageLumber.com

p. 28: Photo courtesy National Spa & Pool Institute

p. 29: Photos: Images provided by Archadeck®, America's outdoor living expert. www.Archadeck.com

p. 30: Photo © Eric Roth

p. 31: (top) Photo © Nicola Browne, Design: Dan Pearson; (bottom) Photo courtesy Victoria Lister Carley, Design: Victoria Lister Carley

p. 32: (top) Photo © Olson Photographic LLC, Architect: Donald William Fairbanks Architect, PC; (bottom) Photo courtesy Mary Dewart, Dewart Design

p. 33: Photo © Rob Karosis, Architect: Rob Whitten, Whitten Architects, Portland, ME, www.whittenarchitects. com

pp. 34-35: Photos © Coles Hairston

CHAPTER 2

p. 36: Photo © Michael Jensen, Architect: Bret Drager, Drager Gould Architects, www.dragergould.com

p. 38 Photo © Eric Roth

p. 39: (top) Photo courtesy www. GardenStructure.com; (bottom) Photo © Chris Giles, Design: David Petersen, Outdoor Structure Company, LLC, Longmont, CO, www.oscdecks.com

p. 40: (top) Photo © Brian Vanden Brink, Design: Polhemus Savery DaSilva Architects Builders; (bottom) Photo © Randy O'Rourke, Architect: Glen Irani Architects, www.glenirani. com

p. 41: (top) Photo by Charles Miller, courtesy Fine Homebuilding, © The Taunton Press, Inc.; (bottom) Photo © Lee Anne White, Design: Michelle Derviss + Miguel Chavez Design + Build

p. 42: (top) Photo © Eric Roth; (bottom) Archadeck

p. 43: Photo © Eric Roth

p. 44: Photo © Lynn Karlin

p. 45: Photo by Charles Bickford, courtesy Fine Homebuilding, © The Taunton Press, Inc.

p. 46: Photos © Eric Roth

p. 48: (photo 1) © Brian Vanden Brink, Architect: James Sterling, AIA, www.sterlingarchitect.com; (photo 2) Photo © Randy O'Rourke, Design: Julie Moir Messervy and Steve Jonas; (photo 3) Photo © Jerry Pavia Photography

p. 49: (photo 4) Photo © Mark Lohman; (photo 5) Photo © Jerry Pavia Photography

p. 50: Photo © www. davidduncanlivingston.com

p. 51: (top) Archadeck®; (bottom) Photo © 2004 Samu Studios, Inc.

pp. 52-53: Photos © Chris Giles, Design: David Petersen, Outdoor Structure Company, LLC, Longmont, CO, www.oscdecks.com

p. 54: (top) Photo © Rob Karosis; Landscape Architect: Charles Hugo; Charles Hugo Landscape Design, Rollinsford, NH, www.charleshugo. com; (bottom) Photo © Olson Photographic LLC; Design: Benchmark Builders

p. 55: Photo © Randy O'Rourke, Design: Maggie Judycki, GreenThemes Inc.

p. 56: (top) Photo © Rob Karosis, Design: Dwight McNeil, Architect, Morris-Day Designers and Builders, www.morris-day.com; (bottom) Photo © Eric Roth

p. 57: Photo © Todd Caverly

pp. 58-59: Photos © Chris Giles, Design: David Petersen, Outdoor Structure Company, LLC, Longmont, CO, www.oscdecks.com

p. 60: Photo © John Gruen

p. 61: Photos © Rob Karosis, Design: Dennis Wedlick Architect, www. dennis-wedlick.com

p. 62: Photo by Kevin Ireton, courtesy of Fine Homebuilding, © The Taunton Press, Inc.

p. 63: Photos: © 2005 Bison Innovative Products/www.BisonIP.com

p. 64: Photo © Anton Grassl

p. 65: (top) Photo © Todd Caverly; (bottom) Photo: © Olson Photographic LLC, Design: Studio DiBerardino, LLC

pp. 66-67: Photos © Randy O'Rourke, Design: Frank Shirley, Frank Shirley Architects, 75 Henry Street, Cambridge, MA 02139, 617-547-3355, www.frankshirleyarchitects.com

CHAPTER 3

p. 68: Photo © www.kenricephoto.com

p. 71: Photo: Roe A. Osborn, courtesy Fine Homebuilding, © The Taunton Press, Inc.

p. 72: (top) Photo © Mark Lohman; (bottom) Photo: © Eric Roth

p. 73: Photo © Olson Photographic LLC

p. 74: (top) Photo © Rob Karosis, Architect: Sam Van Dam, Van Dam Architecture &

Design, Portland, ME www.vandamdesign.com; (bottom) Photo © Todd Caverly

p. 75: Photo © Eric Roth

p. 76: (top) Photo © Rob Karosis, Architect: Rob Whitten, Whitten Architects,

Portland, ME www.whittenarchitects.com; (bottom) Photo © Rob Karosis

p. 79: Photo © Olson Photographic LLC, Design: Four Square Builders

p. 80: (top) Photo © Eric Roth; (bottom) Photo: © Rob Karosis

p. 81: (top) Photo courtesy Inspired House, © The Taunton Press, Inc.; (bottom) Photo: Karen Tanaka, courtesy Inspired House, © The Taunton Press, Inc.

p. 82: (top) Photo courtesy Bobby Parks, Peachtree Decks and Porches, LLC, www.peachtreedecksandporches.com; (bottom) Photo © Lee Anne White, Design: Bobby Parks, Peachtree Decks and Porches, LLC, www.peachtreedecksandporches.com

p. 83: Photo © Lee Anne White, Design: Bobby Parks, Peachtree Decks and Porches, LLC, www.peachtreedecksandporches.com

p. 84: Photo © Cesar Rubio, Design: Peter Pfau, AIA, Pfau Architecture Ltd., pfauarchitecture.com

p. 85: (top) Photo: Image provided by Archadeck®, America's outdoor living expert. www.Archadeck.com; (bottom) Photo © Todd Caverly

pp. 86-87 Photos © Lee Anne White, Design: The Fockele Garden Company

p. 88: (top) Photo © Lee Anne White, Design: Lee Anne White; (bottom) Photo © Todd Caverly

p. 89: Photo © Mark Lohman

p. 90: (photo 1) © Eric Roth; (photo 2) Photo © Chris Giles, Design: David Petersen, Outdoor Structure Company, LLC, Longmont, CO, www.oscdecks.com; (photo 3) Photo © Nicola Brown, Design: Ross Palmer

p. 91: (photo 4) Photo courtesy www.GardenStructure.com; (photo 5) Photo © Eric Roth; (photo 6) Photo courtesy www.GardenStructure.com

p. 92: Photo © Eric Roth

p. 93: Photo: Charles Miller, courtesy Fine Homebuilding, © The Taunton Press, Inc.

p. 94: (left) Photo © Lee Anne White; (right) Photo courtesy www.GardenStructure.com

p. 95: Photo © Eric Roth

p. 96: (photo 1) Photo © Art Gray; (photo 2) Photo © Olson Photographic LLC, Design: Jean Callan King; (photo 3) Photo © Eric Roth

p. 97: (photo 4) Photo courtesy Ernie Sears, Backyard America; (photo 5) Photo courtesy www.GardenStructure.com; (photo 6) Photo © Mark Lohman

pp. 98-99: Photos © Chris Giles, Design: David Petersen, Outdoor Structure Company, LLC, Longmont, CO, www.oscdecks.com

p. 100: Photo © Rob Karosis, Architect: Rob Whitten, Whitten Architects,

Portland, ME www.whittenarchitects.com

p. 101: (top) Photo © Lee Anne White, Design: The Fockele Garden Company; (bottom) Photo: Charles Bickford, courtesy Fine Homebuilding, © The Taunton Press, Inc.

p. 102: (top) Photo © Eric Roth; (bottom) Photo © Randy O'Rourke

pp. 104-105: Photos © Mark Lohman

p. 106: (top) Photo © Rob Karosis, Architect: Sam Van Dam, Van Dam Architecture &

Design, Portland, ME www.vandamdesign.com; (bottom) Photo © Mark Lohman

p. 107: Photos © Eric Roth

p. 108: (top) Photo © ©judywhite/GardenPhotos.com, Design: Natalie Charles; (bottom) Photo © Rob Karosis

p. 109: Picture supplied by AdvantageLumber.com

p. 110: Photo © 2003 carolynbates.com, Architect: Michael Wisniewski, Duncan-Wisniewski Architects, Burlington, VT

p. 111: (top) Photo © davidduncanlivingston.com, Architect: Jean Steinbrecher, AIA, Jean Steinbrecher Architects, Langley, WA, www.jeansteinbrecher.com; (bottom) Photo © Chris Giles, Design: David Petersen, Outdoor Structure Company, LLC, Longmont, CO, www.oscdecks.com

p. 112: (photo 1) Photo © Ken Gutmaker; (photo 2) Photo courtesy Fine Homebuilding, © The Taunton Press, Inc.; (photo 3) Photo © Tria Giovan

p. 113: (photo 4) Photo © Randy O'Rourke; (photo 5) Photo © www.carolynbates.com, Design: Milford Cushman, Cushman & Beckstrom, Inc.; (photo 6) Photo © Chris Giles, Design: David Petersen, Outdoor

Structure Company, LLC, Longmont, CO, www.oscdecks.com

p. 114: Photos: Images provided by Archadeck®, America's outdoor living expert. www.Archadeck.com

p. 115: Photo courtesy Inspired House, © The Taunton Press, Inc.

p. 116: Photo: Image provided by Archadeck®, America's outdoor living expert. www.Archadeck.com

p. 117: (top & center) Photos © Brian Vanden Brink, Design: Carriage House Studio Architects; (bottom) Photo © Lee Anne White, Design: Simply Outdoorz

p. 118: (top) Photo © Eric Roth; (bottom) Photo: Image provided by Archadeck®, America's outdoor living expert. www.Archadeck.com

p. 119: Photo © Kenneth Rice Photography/www.kenricephoto.com, Lighting design: Kichler Lighting

p. 120: Photo courtesy of Aurora Deck Lighting

p. 121: Photo © Eric Roth

p. 122: (photo 1) Photo © Chris Giles, Design: David Petersen, Outdoor Structure Company, LLC, Longmont, CO, www.oscdecks.com; (photo 2) Photo © Lee Anne White, Design: Michelle Derviss + Miguel Chavez Design + Build.; (photo 3) Photo: Image provided by Archadeck®, America's outdoor living expert. www.Archadeck.com; (photo 4) Photo courtesy Ernie Sears, Backyard America

p. 123: (photo 5) Photo by Matthew Borkoski, Courtesy of Trex (CK); (photo 6) Photo © Mark Lohman; (photo 7) Photo: Andrew Wormer, courtesy Fine Homebuilding, © The Taunton Press, Inc.

CHAPTER 4

p. 124: Photo © Todd Caverly

p. 126: Photo © Erik Kvalsvik, Architect: Bohlin Cywinski Jackson, 8 West Market Street, Suite 1200,

Wilkes-Barre, PA 18701, 570-825-8756, www.bcj.com

p. 127: (top) Photo © Erik Kvalsvik, Architect: Michael G. Imber, 111 West El Prado, San Antonio, TX 78212, 210-824-7703, www.michaelgimber. com; (bottom) Photo © Jennifer Cheung and Steven Nilsson, Design: Heather Lenkin of www.lenkindesign. com

p. 128: (top) © davidduncanlivingston. com, Architect: Paul De Groot, 6202 Highland Hills Dr., Austin, TX 78731, 512-345-2228, www.degrootarchitect. com; (bottom) Photo © Rob Karosis, Design: Rob Whitten, Whitten Architecture and Design, Portland, Maine

pp. 130-131: Photos © Chris Giles, Design: David Petersen, Outdoor Structure Company, LLC, Longmont, CO, www.oscdecks.com

p. 132: (top) Photo by Matthew Borkoski, Courtesy of Trex (CK); (bottom) Picture supplied by AdvantageLumber.com

p. 133: Photo © CorrectDeck

pp. 134-135: Photos © Chris Giles, Design: David Petersen, Outdoor Structure Company, LLC, Longmont, CO, www.oscdecks.com

p. 136: (top) Photo © Todd Caverly; (bottom) Photo © Jesse Walker Associates

p. 137: Picture supplied by AdvantageLumber.com

pp. 138-139: Photo: Dan Thornton, courtesy Fine Homebuilding, © The Taunton Press, Inc.

p. 140: Photo by Matthew Borkoski, Courtesy of Trex (CK)

p. 141: Photo by Matthew Borkoski, Courtesy of Trex (CK)

p. 142: Photos: Dan Thornton, courtesy Fine Homebuilding, © The Taunton Press, Inc.

p. 143: (top) Photo by Matthew Borkoski, Courtesy of Trex (CK); (bottom) Photo courtesy CTI Plastics, Ltd.

p. 144: (top) Photo © Jerry Pavia Photography; (bottom) Photo courtesy LockDry

p. 145: Photo © Eric Roth

p. 146: Photo courtesy California Redwood Association

p. 147: Photo: Charles Miller, courtesy Fine Homebuilding, © The Taunton Press, Inc.

p. 148: Photo © Chris Giles, Design: David Petersen, Outdoor Structure Company, LLC, Longmont, CO, www.oscdecks.com

p. 149: Photos © Eric Roth

p. 151: Photos courtesy www. GardenStructure.com

p. 153: (top) Photo © Mark Lohman, Design: Burdge & Assoc.; (right) Photo courtesy Feeney Architectural Products; (bottom) Photo © Jennifer Cheung and Steven Nilsson, Design: Steven Hans Nuetzel, Architect

p. 154: (photos 1 & 3) Photos by Matthew Borkoski, Courtesy of Trex (CK); (photo 2) Photo © Eric Roth

p. 155: (photo 4) Photo courtesy Deckorators; (photo 5) Photo © Eric Roth; (photo 6) Photo: Image provided by Archadeck®, America's outdoor living expert. www.Archadeck.com; (photo 7) Photo by Matthew Borkoski, Courtesy of Trex (CK)

p. 156: (top) Photo © Brian Vanden Brink, Design: Chris Glass, Architect; (bottom) Photo © Jerry Pavia Photography

p. 157: (top) Photo © davidduncanlivingston.com, Design: Brian Mackay-Lyons Architecture, 2188 Gottingen St., Halifax, Nova Scotia, Canada, B3K 3B4, 902-429-1867, www.bmlaud.ca; (bottom) Photo courtesy www.GardenStructure.com

p. 158: Photo © Lee Anne White

p. 159: (top left) Photo © Chris Giles, Design: David Petersen, Outdoor Structure Company, LLC, Longmont, CO, www.oscdecks.com; (top right) Photo © Karla Chronopoulos;

(bottom) Photo by Matthew Borkoski, Courtesy of Trex (CK)

CHAPTER 5

p. 160: Photo: Steve Aitken, courtesy Fine Gardening, © The Taunton Press, Inc.

p. 162: (top) Photo © Eric Roth; (bottom) Photo © Allan Mandell, Design: Linda Ernst

p. 163: Photo © Mark Lohman

p. 165: (top & right) Photos © Todd Caverly; (left) Photo © Randy O'Rourke

p. 166: Photos © Eric Roth

p. 167: Photo © Lee Anne White

p. 168: (top) Photo © Eric Roth; (bottom) Photo © Todd Caverly

p. 169: Photo courtesy O.W. Lee

p. 170: Picture supplied by AdvantageLumber.com

p. 171: (top) Photo © Jerry Pavia Photography; (bottom) Picture supplied by AdvantageLumber.com

p. 172: (top) Photo © Eric Roth; (bottom) Photo © Allan Mandell

p. 173: Photo © Eric Roth

p. 174: (top) Photo © Rob Karosis, Architect: Rob Whitten, Whitten Architects,

Portland, ME www.whittenarchitects. com; (bottom) Photo © Eric Roth

p. 175: (top) Photo © Jerry Pavia Photography; (bottom) Photo © Rob Karosis, Architect: Rebecca Swanston, Swanston & Associates, Baltimore, MD, www.swanstonassociates.com

p. 176: Photo by Matthew Borkoski, Courtesy of Trex (CK)

p. 177: (top) Photo © Chris Giles, Design: David Petersen, Outdoor Structure Company, LLC, Longmont, CO, www.oscdecks.com; (bottom) Photo © Lynn Karlin

p. 178: (top) Photo © Stephanie Phillips/iStockphoto.com; (bottom) Photo © davidduncanlivingston.com

p. 179: Photo © Deidra Walpole Photography, Design: Tony Miller/ Scott Smith

p. 180: Picture supplied by AdvantageLumber.com

p. 181: (top) Photo: Image provided by Archadeck®, America's outdoor living expert. www.Archadeck.com; (bottom) Photo © Lee Anne White, Design: Michelle Derviss + Miguel Chavez Design + Build; (right) Photo © Jessie Walker Associates

p. 182: Photo © Mark Lohman, Design: Grisamore Design

p. 183: Photo © Lee Anne White

p. 184: Photo © Randy O'Rourke

p. 185: (top) Photo © Lee Anne White; (bottom) Photo © Greg Hursley; (right) Photo © Lee Anne White, Design: Joshua Gannon, Range West Gallery

p. 186: Photos © Jerry Pavia Photography

p. 187: Photo © Lee Anne White, Design: The Fockele Garden Company

p. 188: Photo © Eric Roth

p. 189: Photos © Jerry Pavia Photography

p. 190: (top) Photo © Lee Anne White; (bottom) Photo © Jerry Pavia Photography

p. 191: (top) Photo © Deidra Walpole Photography; (bottom & inset) Photos © Lynn Karlin

p. 192: Photo © Olson Photographic LLC

p. 193: (top left & bottom) Photos © Jerry Pavia Photography; (top right) Photo © Lynn Karlin

pp. 194-195: Photos © Chris Giles, Design: David Petersen, Outdoor Structure Company, LLC, Longmont, CO, www.oscdecks.com

INDEX

KITCHEN IDEAS THAT WORK

Beth Veillette
Paperback
$19.95 U.S.

OUTDOOR KITCHEN IDEAS THAT WORK

Lee Anne White
Paperback
$19.95 U.S.

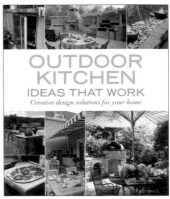

NEW BATHROOM IDEAS THAT WORK

Scott Gibson
Paperback
$19.95 U.S.

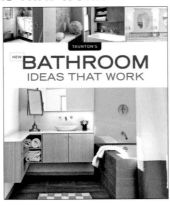

BASEMENT IDEAS THAT WORK

Peter Jeswald
Paperback
$19.95 U.S.

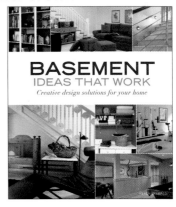

DECORATING IDEAS THAT WORK

Heather J. Paper
Paperback
$21.95 U.S.

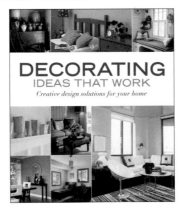